Talk to Me

of related interest

Teach Me With Pictures
40 Fun Picture Scripts to Develop Play and Communication
Skills in Children on the Autism Spectrum
Simone Griffin, Ruth Harris and Linda Hodgdon
Illustrated by Ralph Butler
ISBN 978 1 84905 201 6
eISBN 978 0 85700 632 5

Social Communication Cues for Young Children with
Autism Spectrum Disorders and Related Conditions
How to Give Great Greetings, Pay Cool
Compliments and Have Fun with Friends
Tarin Varughese
ISBN 978 1 84905 870 4
eISBN 978 0 85700 506 9

The Asperkid's (Secret) Book of Social Rules
The Handbook of Not-So-Obvious Social Guidelines
for Tweens and Teens with Asperger Syndrome
Jennifer Cook O'Toole
Illustrated by Brian Bojanowski
ISBN 978 1 84905 915 2
eISBN 978 0 85700 685 1

Strategies for Building Successful Relationships
with People on the Autism Spectrum
Let's Relate!
Brian R. King
Forewords by Liane Holliday Willey and Susan Giurleo
ISBN 978 1 84905 856 8
eISBN 978 0 85700 522 9

60 Social Situations and Discussion Starters to Help Teens on the
Autism Spectrum Deal with Friendships, Feelings, Conflict and More
Seeing the Big Picture
Lisa A. Timms
ISBN 978 1 84905 862 9
eISBN 978 0 85700 468 0

How Everyone on the Autism Spectrum, Young and Old, can...
become Resilient, be more Optimistic, enjoy Humor,
be Kind, and increase Self-Efficacy
A Positive Psychology Approach
June Groden, Ayelet Kantor, Cooper R. Woodard and Lewis P. Lipsitt
Foreword by V. Mark Durand
ISBN 978 1 84905 853 7
eISBN 978 0 85700 520 5

Talk to Me

Conversation Strategies for Parents
of Children on the Autism Spectrum
or with Speech and Language
Impairments

Jessica Kingsley *Publishers*
London and Philadelphia

First published in 2014
by Jessica Kingsley Publishers
73 Collier Street
London N1 9BE, UK
and
400 Market Street, Suite 400
Philadelphia, PA 19106, USA

www.jkp.com

Library of Congress Cataloging in Publication Data
Jones, Heather, 1940-
   Talk to me : a practical guide to conversational therapy for parents of children with
speech and
language difficulties or Asperger syndrome / Heather Jones.
      pages cm
   Includes index.
   ISBN 978-1-84905-428-7 (alk. paper)
   1. Speech therapy for children. 2. Asperger's syndrome in children--Treatment. I.
Title.
   RJ496.S7J65 2014
   618.92'858832--dc23
                                                    2013028716

British Library Cataloguing in Publication Data
A CIP catalogue record for this book is available from the British Library

ISBN 978 1 84905 428 7
eISBN 978 0 85700 898 5

Printed and bound in Great Britain

To four strong women who supported
me throughout the writing of this book:
my sister, Eleanor; my mother, Peggy; my
mother-in-law, Iris; and my helpmate, Floss.

Contents

Part II Developing Social Skills, Life Skills and Independence

Preface

I am the mother of a boy on the autism spectrum, Jamie Bennetto.

Jamie has Asperger syndrome and a debilitating speech and language impairment. In 2005 he was assessed by a speech pathologist, who found that his expressive language was in the 0.2 percentile. That means that of 100 boys of Jamie's age, 99.8 per cent of them could speak better than he could. His language was also 'profoundly impaired', being in the first percentile. She also remarked that 'his responses to many test items showed a limited understanding of the appropriate language to use in social situations and [he had] difficulty in formulating responses using the appropriate form'.

When Jamie was four, I took him to a special course for oppositional kids because I had to drag him kicking and screaming to have a bath. At the age of seven he was suspended from school for kicking the teacher's car door in because she wouldn't take him on a fishing trip. (The damage cost me hundreds of dollars.) I constantly had to get plumbers in to fix our drains, which were blocked from the stones Jamie was throwing down them, and nothing I said or did would persuade him not to do it. His primary school teacher was dreading his first days at school because she knew she wouldn't be able to cope with him (and that was in Special Education!).

Finally I heard about a specialist school for speech- and language-impaired children, and they did the assessments I mentioned above. Jamie enrolled there in July 2005 when he was ten. But even there the problems continued. He once raged so much at After School Care that he smashed the steel pool cue in two. He broke their table tennis bat. He stormed out of lessons. He used the 'f*** word' many times when he was upset (and at the time that seemed to be every day). They had a zero tolerance policy for swear words at the school and I was called in every time he swore to take him home. This made me very popular with my workplace.

His paediatrician recommended Ritalin. I prevaricated. What good were drugs going to do for him? At home he was calm unless Caitlin, his sister, got upset. It was only the provocation and conflict that arose when he misunderstood his peers or teachers that drove him to become a blistering, loud-mouthed sailor.

Nothing I said to him seemed to have any effect. True, he was genuinely sad afterwards and he wrote many letters of apology to the school, to teachers, to carers, to fellow students he'd hit or abused, but we kept going over the same ground again and again. He was very sorry. He'd never do it again. He'd be a better boy tomorrow.

Eight months after he joined the school, in March 2006, I stumbled across a way to connect with Jamie. It happened by accident and I'll never know what led me to this new way of talking to him, but, for the first time, I was making sense to him and he was making sense to me. Since then, through many, many conversations and experiments, my methods have expanded, developed and blossomed. From conversation, we moved to socialising, behaviour patterns and life skills. Now, six years later, I have a different boy to lead through life. This is the story of that journey.

I have written this book in the hope that other parents and carers can benefit from the path that I have travelled with my son and the discoveries we have made along the way. The book is written in two parts: the first and larger part is devoted to my efforts at teaching Jamie conversation – a skill he was woefully lacking in – and the second part shows the social and life skills that developed as a result of his being able to hold a conversation.

Since the publication of the *Diagnostic and Statistical Manual of Mental Disorders, Fifth Edition (DSM-5)* in May 2013, 'Asperger syndrome' no longer exists as a distinct diagnosis and has been subsumed by 'Autism Spectrum Disorder' (ASD). However, as Jamie was diagnosed with Asperger syndrome and his diagnosis stands, I have chosen to use this term. If your child has been diagnosed with ASD, you can read 'Asperger syndrome' as 'high-functioning autism'.

If you enjoy this book and would like to contact me about any aspect of parenting or caring for a child with autism and/or speech and language impairments, you can reach me on milkwoodproperty@gmail.com. I wish you all the best in the demanding yet joyous challenge of bringing up one of our magical children and look forward to hearing from you.

PART I
Working on Conversation

CHAPTER 1

Increasing Vocabulary is Not Enough!

It was clear by the time Jamie was two years old that his speech was delayed. I had had two girls before Jamie and was told many times that boys develop their language skills later than girls, that Einstein didn't speak until he was three, and that it was anxiety on my part that prompted concern in this area.

But his speech didn't improve. Where my girls had an active vocabulary of 300 words at the age of two, Jamie's vocabulary languished at 20 words for months and months. I was worried about him and, at that stage, had no idea that this language delay was due to Asperger's. So, when things hadn't improved by the time he was four, I took him to a speech therapist. Over the years he saw three different private speech therapists and attended two workshops offered externally through a private speech and language school.

This is an extract from my diary after our first session with a new speech therapist:

> Today was our first session at speech therapy. It seemed to me a lesson in how not to do it. First, you stick a child in a strange room across a desk from a stranger who fires questions at him about a cartoon character he has no interest in and she then hides the answers from him. Second, you put a whole array of attractive toys right next to him and forbid him to touch them! You

then proceed to teach him vocabulary he's hardly likely to use like 'dump truck' and test his ability to remember these arbitrary terms by giving him instructions and not even showing him these things in real life or on video or in colour.

Jamie showed two alternating reactions: he fidgeted and scowled or he went off to lah-lah land and tuned out.

But the speech therapist was only following my instructions. I had told her that Jamie had problems with grammar and vocabulary, so throughout all these and other sessions she concentrated on the mechanics of grammar (syntax) and the enlargement of Jamie's vocabulary (lexical items). He did endless exercises on reflexive pronouns, for instance, 'They wash themselves. He hurts himself. I see myself' and naming obscure pieces of equipment from pictures ('bulldozer', 'bobcat').

After one three-day workshop of intensive speech work when Jamie was nine, he came home with a scrapbook of his work. It contained all the sports played at the Olympics. This wasn't even close to what I wanted. I didn't want him to be able to name 25 Olympic sports or even ten. I wanted him to have a meaningful conversation with his grandmother over the phone. I wanted him to answer a shop-keeper's query on his health and respond with 'And how are you?'. I wanted him know the social value of language.

The question stuck in my mind for years: How do you improve someone's language who hasn't the faintest idea that it's important to communicate? How do you get a blind man to discuss the colour red? Jamie was not just missing the wherewithal – he was missing the point. Dealing with the symptoms (his lack of grammar and vocabulary) wasn't approaching the problem. I had to find some other way into his world…

Tip

Children on the autism spectrum with speech and language difficulties need language explained to them. They need to understand that they are obliged to speak on many occasions and they need to have some cues as to what they can say from the vast choice available to any speaker at any time. (They also have to learn that their pet topic is not the way to converse properly.)

If we can help them in those choices, they can learn the rules to any two-way conversation, and if they learn those rules, after a time they can come to hold a meaningful conversation.

CHAPTER 2

How to Get Your Child Talking

In 2004, when Jamie was ten, I was sitting in the car driving him from school. It was a common occurrence and we sat there in silence as the landscape passed us by. Again and again, I wondered what was going through his head. Again and again, I struggled with the idea – how could I connect with him?

That day I was sick – I'd come home early from work – and I was frustrated… Frustrated by not being able to talk with my son.

I am a writer of dozens of schoolbooks for learners of English as a Second Language. I have a post-graduate degree in English, have worked as a lecturer in Communication at university, and have learnt three languages other than English. My life is writing and my love is words.

Here I was with my dearest boy and I just couldn't talk to him. His answers, if they came at all, were monosyllabic. He just wasn't interested in talking. He laughed a lot and loved watching funny cartoons. He was often in trouble, mainly for throwing temper tantrums, but he was a caring boy. I knew he had a lovely soul, but I couldn't reach it.

I sat with my hands on the wheel, looking at the road ahead… Driving and feeling awful – physically and emotionally.

Suddenly I said loudly, 'Right, Jamie. You are going to speak. And we are going to have a conversation!'

He was quite alarmed. I never spoke with such force unless I was angry with him. He looked at me sharply.

'We'll start with this: Jamie, I was sick today.'

There was a pause. You see, to a child with Asperger's or autism, a statement like that needs no follow up. It's not a question, so it doesn't require a reply. It's not an instruction, so it doesn't need any action from him. It's simply a statement. It was only the tone I used that showed I wanted something from him. Something I'd never demanded before – a reply.

There was no response.

I spoke again: 'I was sick today.' Pause. 'Now it's your turn.'

He looked a bit pained and shuffled in his seat.

'I was sick today. I came home from work,' I said tightly.

There was another pause and then I heard the magical words: 'Did you eat something?'

I laughed and laughed. I almost cried, there in the traffic in the middle of the busy road.

'No, Jamie,' I said, 'I didn't eat something bad. It wasn't my tummy that was sick. I had a headache.'

'Oh.'

'That was very good, Jamie. Very good. I'm really pleased with you.'

Having seen this little glimpse of what Jamie could do, I ploughed on: 'Now it's your turn. I said I was sick. You asked if I'd eaten something. Now you're the speaker again. It's your turn.' I looked at him expectantly. He waited. Then fidgeted, looked out of the window. But I went on: 'Jamie. I'm waiting.'

After a pause, he said: 'Are you sick now?'

'Great work, Jamie!! No, I'm not sick any longer. I'm feeling much better. Thank you.'

Jamie smiled hesitantly. This mother who hungered for communication and demanded something in speech was a little strange to him. It was truly odd for him to be expected to volunteer anything. Before, I had been content with 'Yes', 'No', 'Please' and 'Thank you'. Now I wanted more for some strange reason.

And this was the beginning of our experiments in conversation. And had we but known, it was the beginning of something else – the beginning of a lifetime of dialogue...

Tip

Be specific about what you want from your child. Say things like: 'It's your turn. I want to hear you say something now.' 'You're the speaker and I'm the listener.'

Most parents want to be listened to but we also need to be spoken to. And the first step is to make our demands clear and polite – we want our children to practise, experiment and eventually engage in a real conversation.

CHAPTER 3

Demanding a Conversation with Your Child

When I started a real conversation with Jamie, I began with these words: 'Jamie, we're going to have a conversation.'

It was as simple as that. I was telling him what was going to happen. I was giving him the purpose of our exchange. I was the mummy. I was calling the shots.

I wondered afterwards if such a long word like 'conversation' could be meaningful to him and whether he'd have problems pronouncing it. After all, his vocabulary was painfully small and I doubted he could understand abstract nouns. And then I thought, well, he has no problem with 'Reactivation' and 'Transformation' from Dragonball-Z, so why should he baulk at pronouncing 'conversation'. It quickly became a keyword.

In fact, it soon became a term to be hated. Jamie went through a stage of resenting me saying, 'Let's have a conversation'. He turned his head away and sighed or said, 'Oh, no, you always say "Conversation".' I sympathised with him – after all, it's easy to say, 'Let's have a conversation', but it's so difficult to take part in one when you lack the vocabulary and comprehension. But he had to realise that there was an expectation of him to do something.

So stating what was necessary came first – he knew 'conversation' was 'talking' and, for some reason, his mother was expecting him to do just that. But how? Exactly what did I want?

I realised pretty quickly that Jamie had no idea how to start or continue a conversation in the regular way. When you're a mother in this situation, you begin by asking questions to involve your child in giving the answers. But if I asked, 'Do you like this?' he would just say 'Yes' or 'No'.

'Do you like pizza?'

'Yes,' he replied.

'Have you done this puzzle?'

'No.'

'Are you going to put that in the wash?'

'Yes.'

This is the classic and simple way to ask questions, but unless you have a practised interviewee, you get one-word answers. Conversation is made up of more than 'Yes' and 'No'. So, the next stage in getting Jamie to emulate a real conversation was to demand more of him.

First, I tried, 'Can you tell me more?' That just led to scowls and a curt 'No', which left us just where we started. So then I'd ask more specific questions, but ones starting with the 'Wh-' and 'How' question words. These lead to more fruitful exchanges.

'Did you play soccer today?'

'Yes.'

'Who was on your team?'

'Daniel and Nicholas.'

'Where did you play?'

'On the oval.'

'How did you do?'

'Do?'

'Did you win?'

'We winned.'

That kind of exchange is much more useful and, what is more, I could then summarise the information in a meaningful whole that Jamie could use to tell someone else about the soccer game.

'So you played soccer today with Daniel and Nicholas on the oval and you won. Is that right?'

'Yes,' he would say, smiling.

Tips

Try to avoid 'Yes'/'No' questions when talking to your child. They give the child the opportunity to give monosyllabic answers. If you do ask 'Yes'/'No' questions, demand further explanation or expansion by your child. Ask them prompt questions which will give them some idea of what to say. 'Can you tell me why?' is a good leading question, or just 'Tell me about it'.

After you have gathered a certain amount of information from a section of conversation, repeat it back to your child so that they can learn how to piece together parts of an experience to make a conversational whole.

Set out what you expect from your child. Lay the ground rules for the conversation. Be explicit: 'Ask me a question.' 'It's your turn.' 'I'm not very interested in trains/cars/puzzles/ *The Simpsons* today. Let's talk about school or what we'll do tonight.'

In the end you don't mind what they say, as long as it's meaningful and follows on from the previous remark. They can ask a question, repeat a word, make a joke, start their own conversation, whatever, but they have to take part in the game of conversation.

CHAPTER 4

It's Never Too Late to Start Encouraging Conversation

When I first started working with Jamie in this way, I felt I'd missed so many of his fertile, receptive years – years when I could have been encouraging him, correcting him, opening him up to the method, means and purpose of communication.

I regretted the fact that the door had only opened to me when he was ten years old. What could we have achieved together if I'd started when he was six or four or even two? There was so much water already under the bridge.

But I comforted myself with this thought – my two girls developed their language abilities so quickly, there was barely time to register that they'd learnt how to conjugate verbs before they were generating complex sentences and writing discursive essays. They flew through their language learning. But with Jamie I've been able to mark the advent of each new step along the way. He's blossomed slowly and each new petal is remarkable and welcomed for the very reason that it's delayed and marked. It's so clear when he now knows that a pause in the conversation means he's required to supply an answer or make a contribution. I feel so triumphant when he makes a very ordinary rejoinder, like 'That's nice', which I know has come after months of reminders. And it's such a victory when he overcomes his anger or tells me proudly he's a 'person' now.

This victory has been a long time coming, but it's based to a large extent on the encouragers I have used to modify Jamie's behaviour since he was about 10 or 11. I always had it in my mind that it was better to encourage a child to behave well rather than to punish them for behaving badly.

And there are so many ways to encourage a child: to provide treats, such as food; to reward them with activities; to lavish them with your attention; to give them money or presents (I don't like to give food or money). The most effective one I have found is to give praise.

Jamie learnt the word 'mature' from the covers of DVDs he wasn't allowed to watch – MA For Mature Persons Only. He knew this meant that you had to be almost an adult and responsible. In fact, he used the word 'person' in a particular way, so that on his sister's fifteenth birthday card he wrote: 'You are a Person now.'

So whenever he did something good, by acting well or resisting the temptation to act up, I told him, 'You're being very mature'. He would swell with pride and say, 'Am I?' And I then used the points system (see Chapter 6 Finding a Reward System That Your Child Can Verbalise) to put it into numbers for him. 'You're an 11 today.' 'Am I?' 'Yes, you…', and then I would specifically list the things he'd done well. By choosing to make the reward a verbal one (praise), I was underlining the importance of language. It was words that would reward him; it was through communication that he could measure his achievements.

Starting conversational therapy with your child – at whatever age – means that there is simply a longer period of minor achievements and each one will be recognised, if not by the school or his friends, at least by you.

Tips

Don't worry about when you start conversational therapy with your child. It's never too late, and however far behind they are, the greater the number of achievements that lie along the way ahead.

Use the Appendix at the back of the book to gauge where your child is in their language skills, and proudly enter the date for each passing milestone.

CHAPTER 5

Talking About a Diagnosis

After working with Jamie for a while, I realised the truth about why I wanted him to become a conversationalist – because he was on the autism spectrum; he had Asperger syndrome. But how was I to tell him? I didn't want to make him think he was strange, odd or abnormal. Yet I wanted him to understand why he had difficulties and to be able to overcome his natural frustration with his ability to communicate.

Then the answer appeared at just the right time: I read a book called *Freaks, Geeks and Aspergers Syndrome* by a boy with autism called Luke Jackson. He was 13 when he wrote it and he writes about his life. In it he made it perfectly clear that he was glad when his mother told him he had autism. (I think this was around the age of 11.) He said he wished she'd told him earlier and that he felt very strongly that parents should tell their children of their condition as soon as possible.

I took this as a sign to tell Jamie that he had Asperger's. I told him as simply as I could: 'You're not very good at conversation. That's why I want you to practise it. The reason you're not very good is because you have Asperger's. That means your brain works in a special way. You find it hard to listen and understand. So I'm helping you and we'll talk together.'

'I can talk,' he said.

'Yes, you can talk, Jamie, but you can't communicate.'

'Like conversation?'

'Yes, like conversation. The conversations we've been having. I've had to teach you how to have a conversation. And you're coming on very well.'

Jamie took this thought away and pondered on it. Then, a few days later, he asked, 'Is my blood different?'

I didn't quite understand what he meant but I realised this related back to having Asperger's.

'No,' I said, 'your blood isn't different. Your brain is slightly different. You just find it difficult to talk and understand.'

'I have Asperger's.'

'Yes, and when you're older you can read about it.'

Since then we have had many conversations about Asperger's. Sometimes he gets angry about it and says it's not fair. Then I encourage him by telling him how far he's come.

Now he's 16 and saying, 'I'm growing out of Asperger's, aren't I?' It's heartbreaking to tell him that no, he's not growing out of the condition. But he's learning to live with it and developing his conversation skills all the time.

About three years after this, when Jamie was 19, I was reading a book called *Be Different* by John Elder Robison. John Robison has Asperger syndrome and is now a successful middle-aged businessman. He writes of the anxiety and difficulties he had growing up.

As I was reading, I started to talk to Jamie about this man. Mr Robison calls himself an 'Aspie' and I used this term in my conversations with Jamie. Jamie took to the word easily and seemed to like comparing himself to Robison.

At the end of the book, there's an Appendix based on *The Diagnostic and Statistical Manual of Mental Disorders (DSM IV)*, a checklist for doctors on all kinds of diseases and conditions. Robison provides two lists for the confirmation of Asperger's:

1. Doctors say at least two behaviours have to apply of the following four to diagnose Asperger's:

   (a) The person might have difficulty with non-verbal behaviours like eye-to-eye gaze or reading facial expressions, body postures and gestures.

   (b) The person might not be able to make friends with kids their own age.

   (c) People with Asperger's often seem self-absorbed or uninterested in other people.

   (d) People with Asperger's don't mirror other people's expressions, such as smiling.

2. And at least one of the following four:

   (a) The person must have an 'all-encompassing preoccupation' (e.g. dinosaurs or washing machines).

   (b) The person may be stuck on 'non-functional rituals or routines'.

   (c) The person might display stereotyped and repetitive motor mannerisms, such as rocking.

   (d) The person might be preoccupied with parts of objects.

Jamie had all the first group of criteria when he was younger and an 'all-encompassing preoccupation' with films from the second.

Anyway, I decided to read these out aloud to him and to go through them and work out how much he had improved.

I recited the criteria in very simple terms:

- 'Aspies don't make eye contact' (we'd covered 'eye contact' many times). Then I congratulated him on overcoming his eye-contact problems.

- 'Aspies find it difficult to make friends.' Then I explained that he *was* able to make friends (though I didn't say he didn't know what to say to them unless there was a planned activity for them).

- I said that he was no longer self-absorbed ('thinking about yourself and not others' was what I said to him).

- I said that he *did* show he cared by his facial expressions.

- I also added another criterion which I have noticed a lot in Jamie – his startle reflex at sudden noises or even his inability to bear low noises in another room, such as humming or the radio. 'You get upset at loud noises. And that's a difficulty you still have.'

He was really interested in this 'checklist' of Yes/No standards and keen to see how far he'd come. He nodded and listened attentively.

I thought no more of it until later at dinner, when he sat next to me and leant forward.

'I'm not going to get upset at noises any more. When my sister Caitie starts humming, I'm not going to get angry at her. She's doing it because she's happy.' I smiled. 'And when Nanna plays the piano,' he said, 'I'm going to stay in the same room because it makes her happy.'

And he has been as good as his word.

Tips

As soon as the symptoms of Asperger's or autism spectrum disorder become obvious to your child, tell them about the condition. It may upset them, but it's better to know why ideas are confused in your brain and why you can't follow a simple conversation with your friends.

Wait until your child asks a related question then take the opportunity to explain as clearly as possible. Alternatively, you can mention it when 'debriefing' an explosion or temper tantrum.

Don't burden your child with unnecessary information or try to explain in detail the symptoms of the condition until they're ready. Keep it simple and positive.

CHAPTER 6

Finding a Reward System That Your Child Can Verbalise

In October 2004, when Jamie was nine, we were over with my daughter, Becca and her boyfriend, Ross and I was telling them how good Jamie had been. Becca is my eldest daughter and some 18 years older than Jamie. She has always acted like a second mother to her younger siblings. While I was talking to Becca, Ross was trying to make conversation with Jamie. He asked how good he'd been. Jamie didn't really have a reply. Ross turned to me.

'How many points out of ten was he?' asked Ross.

'Oh,' I said, 'he was eight out of ten. Very good.'

Jamie beamed. We didn't mention the points again.

Then, a few weeks later we were driving home in the car and Jamie was kicking and screaming. I can't remember over what now. His feet were bashing the dashboard and he was threatening to get out of the moving car. I turned on him and shouted, 'If Ross asked me how many points you were now – I'd say two. Two out of ten!'

Jamie immediately went quiet. He sat thinking, cogitating. We drove on. I was so surprised that anything had stopped the outburst.

A few minutes later he asked, 'How many points am I now?'

'Oh,' I said, 'you're six out of ten. You're not shouting. You're not screaming. You've put your legs down. You're not banging the dashboard any more. You're six out of ten.'

As we pulled into the driveway a few minutes later, he asked me again, 'How many points now?' And I gave him eight out of ten.

That was the beginning of the points system for us. I had often been told that children like to have rewards to encourage them and I tried using stickers for a few weeks when he was seven, but he had no interest in stars or labels. Suddenly – with the points system – he had a great sense of reward from marks out of ten.

It was a very haphazard system at first. I gave him points only when we remembered it. Then I started writing it on the calendar and then before I knew it, he was reminding me to write it up so he could look at it and show visitors. At first I was adding up points and taking away points throughout the day, but that got too complicated. I decided to adopt a simple way of doing it – he started with ten points each day, then he got one point off for anything naughty he did and one extra point for anything good. In theory, that meant that he could earn more than 10 points in a day.

Six months later we were using the points system religiously and we followed it until he was 18. It didn't stop the bad behaviour straightaway, but it gave him a gauge as to how bad his behaviour was. When he shouted coarse language at people, he lost five points; forgetting to unpack the dishwasher was one point; sitting quietly through a TV show I was interested in was plus five points.

The secondary advantage of this system was that it brought the calendar into our lives in a big way. Now I could write down Jamie's upcoming events on something tangible: his sports day, my trips away, our holidays.

Also, I suddenly had another weapon in my armoury. When he broke the snooker cue, he lost his computer and video rights for a week as well as five points; he also had to write a letter of apology to the carers and pay for the replacement cue out of his pocket money.

Pretty soon Jamie was getting tens regularly and every night he said to me, 'Don't forget my points.'

The points system worked brilliantly and continued for another six years. I told Jamie when it would end – when he was 18. I told him a young man doesn't have points awarded to him by his mother. Then he would be a 'mature person'.

Tip

Find some measuring stick that your child can recognise and believe in, knowing that it is fairly used. For some children, it's stickers on a chart; for others, it's Tic Tacs, but for Jamie it was points. When he could see them up there, he knew how good a day he'd had. And when we got to the end of the month and he'd got more than three 11 out of 10s, he got an overnight DVD.

CHAPTER 7

Using a Diary as a Conversation Catalyst

Perhaps you already keep a diary. Perhaps you've thought you'd never keep one regularly if you started, but I strongly recommend beginning a diary and writing down anything of note about your child. It's amazing how quickly time passes and you forget their activities and thoughts, so it's great to have a reminder.

Don't use a regular diary – it will intimidate you if you aren't in the habit of writing already. Keep a loose-leaf notebook by your bedside and write down daily events including:

- your child's thoughts

- your child's actions

- your child's words

- your and other people's reactions.

Not only will this help you in reflecting on your child's achievements, it can also point you in the direction of where you need to focus your attention. When I look back at the diary I've kept on Jamie for the last five years, I can chart his progress. (I must add that I only wrote in it once every couple of weeks so it wasn't onerous.)

At first, in order to have something to write in the diary, I asked Jamie what he did at school. After two or three days of non-committal responses, I decided to change tack.

'Name three things you did today.' That stumped him, so I helped him. 'Well, I know you had soccer today. So what happened at soccer?'

'We won.'

'That's great. So you won at soccer.'

'Yes. And Nicholas got hurted.'

'Oh, did he trip?'

'Trip?'

'Did he fall over something?'

'Yes.'

'And did you kick the ball or were you in goal?'

'I kicked the ball.'

'So today you played a game of soccer and you kicked the ball, but Nicholas tripped up and hurt himself but in the end you won!'

I always love these conversations because I tease out the salient details of his day and then weave them together into a mini-story. It makes him absorb correct grammar and teaches him a sense of narrative.

Later in the diary days, I wrote, 'Jamie got bored with "What three things did you do today?"' So then I started on tastes, like 'What is your favourite game?' 'What is your favourite subject?' 'What is your favourite film?' and so on. Often these rather banal answers took us into unknown areas.

'I like *Terminator* because it has themes. What are themes?' He knew the word from the warnings on the video cases, but wanted to know more about it.

There then followed a monologue by me, which I'm sure Jamie didn't understand (I know he didn't because the same question recurred throughout the following years), but the conversation did actually chart unknown and unexpected territory.

So if you're thinking of writing a diary, use it as a catalyst in your conversations to find out more about your child and their thoughts. Be gentle and generous with yourself and your child. It shouldn't be a test but, if you're persistent (as opposed to nagging), you can improve your son or daughter's output and receptive understanding.

Tips

Watch the film *Seven Up!* – a marvellous British documentary charting the lives of a dozen children every seven years in their lives into middle-age. The first one includes conversations with the kids and the questions can be starting points to stories, discussion or advice: 'What kinds of food do you like?', 'What will you do after school?', 'Where do you want to live?', and of course, 'Why?'

Alternatively, have your child write a sentence or two in their own words – it helps with reinforcing the language and nails down the experience. Here's an example:

Monday 12th of November 11, 2007 NEWS.

I have been going to skates 'n' blade with my mum on the 11th of November.

We go on Sunday afternoon.

there is always lots of people at skates 'n' blade and they play loud music and I am getting better and better.

it cost $10.

CHAPTER 8

Teaching Your Child How to Ask 'Wh-' Questions

One of the most basic ways of keeping a conversation going, or even starting a conversation, is to ask questions. It's the equivalent of lobbing a ball at someone for them to return metaphorically to you, and so begins the game of conversation.

The problem that our children have is that they don't realise this. They have no conception that communication is a two-way street or a building block in the construction of relationships between themselves and other people. So we have to make it clear what is expected of them and we can do this through modelling questions.

'Nathan wasn't at school today.'

Silence.

'Now it's your turn... Ask a "Wh-" question.'

Silence.

'You can ask, "*What* was wrong with him?" or "*Where* was he?"'

'What was wrong with him?'

'He went to the dentist... That's very good, Jamie. You thought of a "Wh-" question. Let's do another... Grandma is coming over on Sunday... Now think of a "Wh-" question.'

Silence.

'Why? Now you go on.'

'Why is she coming?'

'Good, very good... She's coming to bring you a present.'

'A present?'

'Yes. And I think you'd like to know *what* sort of present. Or *what* it is.'

'What it is.'

'We don't say, "What it is", we say, "What is it?"'

'What is it?'

'What is it? I don't know. But I think for a boy who's doing so well at his questions, it'll be a special present.'

And so the conversation continued. Every time Jamie used a question word (even when prompted or cued with the complete question), I praised him and repeated the question in full. Also, I corrected any grammatical mistakes by saying, 'We don't say "X", we say "Y".'

There's been a lot of discussion about whether grammar should be corrected. Apparently, native speakers of all countries rarely correct their children's speech patterns, but I have deliberately chosen to correct and model the right responses for Jamie. I figure it makes him realise that there are acceptable and non-acceptable language forms.

Anyway, I did find Jamie caught onto the meaning of 'Wh-' questions pretty quickly. He was slower to use them spontaneously in his own speech, but with a bit of prompting, he could usually find an appropriate question for a situation.

Tips

'Wh-' questions start with: 'Who', 'What', 'When', 'Where', 'Why' and 'How'. Think of as many possible questions that can be formed in response to a statement by you and then choose the simplest to provide an opener for your child. For young children, it is probably best to stick to 'What', 'When' and 'Where', since 'Who' and 'How' don't sound like 'Wh-' questions (they make the 'H' sound) and 'Why' is pretty sophisticated conceptually.

Think of using the questions to describe the scenes you pass in the street. For example, 'There's the postman... Let's think of a 'Wh-' question... 'Where...?' or 'Look at that car... What colour is it?' It will enliven conversations in traffic and reinforce the concept of asking follow-up questions.

CHAPTER 9

Teaching Turn-Taking in Conversation

Dr Temple Grandin, a well-known expert on autism, spoke of what it is like to have autism when taking part in regular conversations. She explained that it was like watching a game of tennis. Where you knew there were rules, but you couldn't work them out yourself.

From that first day, when Jamie was ten and I demanded a response from him, I have learnt to spell out one of the most basic rules of conversation: turn-taking.

People take turns in conversation. One person speaks, then the next one. Sometimes there are overlaps, and sometimes one person interrupts another, and at other times encouragers are used by the listener to show that they appreciate the speaker's words and understand them, but overall the flow is 'give' then 'take'. And in taking turns, at any given time, one is acting as either the speaker or the listener.

Turn-taking in conversation is as natural to us as the concepts of listener and speaker, but to Jamie it was as alien and difficult to him as naming the stars in the sky. He had no grasp of the concept and used to repeat lines from films at the most inappropriate times. I remember going out to a fancy restaurant one day when he was about five, and he turned to the waitress and said happily, 'Get a life.' He smiled at her at the same time and luckily she didn't catch what he said, but I was acutely embarrassed.

To begin with, I taught Jamie the concepts 'listener' and 'speaker' directly. 'I'm the speaker now and I want to say this...' Then, 'Now, I'm the listener and you're the speaker. It's your turn.'

It became a game. Of course, it was difficult for him to come up with something on his own. He needed guidance: 'You can ask me how my day was. Or you can tell me more about your day,' I said. When I started the conversation about my health, I gave him prompts: 'You can ask me how I am now. Say "How are you, mummy?"' 'Or you can say, "Are you better now?"' I modelled the sentences he should use.

Every schoolchild seems to be reluctant to talk about their day. I've found I have more chance of an answer, if I ask a specific question: 'What did you do in sports/maths/music today?' This is where it's good to know their timetable so that you can bring that knowledge to the conversation. Or: 'What did you learn today?' Or: 'Tell me three things about your day.'

I discovered this last one by accident and it has been a gem. When I first started asking Jamie this, he kept saying, 'Oh, it's so hard. I can't think in my mind.' So I asked him leading questions, such as: 'What did you see?' 'What did you hear?' 'Was anyone sick today?' 'Did you get mad with anyone?'

After a few weeks of asking the 'three things' question, he'd sigh and screw up his face. 'Oh, mum, why do you always say that?' He began to resent it, but I didn't change the question – I changed my manner.

I'd run up to him at After School Care and greet him beaming, saying, 'I've been waiting to hear about your three things. I can't wait any longer. What three things happened?' And his attitude changed, too!

I have notebooks full of his three incidents per day... things like: Jason and he played soccer; his teacher was away; they had formal lunch; Daniel got angry; the builders are digging up the playground. I treasured each and every one of these anecdotes as little emblems of the progress he was making.

To help your child 'get' the concept of turn-taking, you can use a card or dice or some special object which you exchange between you as you speak and listen. The speaker gets the object (e.g. a bauble):

'I think I'm going to make a cake today. Would you like to help?' Then pass the bauble to your child, saying, 'Now it's your turn.' And using the bauble can include other members of the family so that for short periods of time, you play 'Pass the Talking Bauble' or whatever you want to call it.

Using the tips on helping your child to phrase questions from the previous chapter, you can introduce cue sentences like 'Ask me a "Wh-" question' and so on. This will help them get an idea of what to say.

This is one of the most powerful tools in your child's development. If they can understand the turn-taking, the ebb and flow of a dialogue – their responsibilities as well as their 'place' in an interchange – they are half-way to learning the turn-taking rules of social interaction and taking their rightful place in that grand game we call 'conversation'.

Tips

The first thing you have to do with your child is to make sure they know there are rules in conversation and the primary rule is that we take turns. When a cavernous silence opens up, don't immediately say something to fill the silence. Leave the silence for a while and explain: 'Now there's silence. See if you can say something or ask a question.'

Make sure your child knows that they have a responsibility in conversing. On the other hand, they also have a responsibility to involve you in what they're saying and you should not be slow in saying, 'Okay, now it's my turn' if necessary.

Know your child's timetable at school so that you can ask specific questions to start a conversation.

Use a 'Talking Bauble' to signify the speaker at any one time. Place it in your child's hand, saying: 'Now it's your turn.' Soon, you'll be able to hand it over without words and your child will know it's time to speak.

CHAPTER 10

Teaching Your Child to Be an Active Listener

Active listening is an art. It requires sensitivity and understanding. Yet our children lack the very basics in comprehension. How can they learn the delicate movement of a conversation that can take the speakers anywhere?

Ironically, active listening at its best is not just the passive skill of listening, but choosing from a selection of cue words that encourage the speaker to continue or that add your own experience to the conversation.

Here are three key strategies you can teach your child:

- Repeat keywords as a question.

- Ask follow-up questions with 'Wh-' or 'Yes'/'No' questions.

- Contribute their own ideas.

Keywords

As I said earlier, people with Asperger's or autism are less likely to respond to statements such as 'I'm going home now'. They are not being asked a question or asked to do something, so they feel it doesn't require a response. If your child has this reaction to statements, repeat keywords, like 'home'.

Here is a conversation I had with Jamie:

'We're going to see a film on Saturday.'

Pause.

'Jamie.'
Pause.
'Now it's your turn. So you can say "Film?"'
'Film?'
'That's right. We're seeing *The Simpsons*. Is that good? Do you like that?'
'Yes.'

Follow-up questions

Once you've taught your child the 'Wh-' questions, you can phrase your own follow-up questions and ask them to repeat them.

'I've just bought a book... Now ask me a "Wh-" question.'
'Why?'
'That's a bit difficult. But because I want to read it. It's about a man in Asia who's very good to the people there... Ask me about the book again... Ask me a "What" question.'
'What...is the book?'
'Very good, Jamie. The book is called *Three Cups of Tea*.'

Contributing their own ideas

When you do ask your child questions, they are likely to give monosyllabic answers (in fact, many children do) – 'Yes' or 'No'. Try to get them to expand these words and take an active part in the conversation. Just tell them what you want.

'Do you like doing puzzles?'
'Yes.'
'Tell me more.'
Those three little words opened up a chink in Jamie's reserve.
'Yes, I do like them.'
'Say why you do.'
'I like them because...er...because they're nice.'
'Good, Jamie.'

Developing listening skills

I started on helping Jamie's listening by taking the bull by the horns and demanding a response.

'Ask me a question about my life,' I said.

There was a long silence. 'Do you like some boats?' he asked hesitantly.

'Yes, I do like boats,' I replied, giving him the correct grammatical version. 'I like them because they travel on the sea. I like the sea. What about you? Do you like boats?'

'Yes,' he said.

'Can you tell me more?' I prompted.

Silence.

'Can you tell me *why* you like boats?'

'Because they have seats,' he replied rather ambiguously.

'That's great! You like boats because they have seats. See - I listened to you.'

After a while, I began to use this 'expansion' technique in a lot of different situations. Instead of just answering 'Yes' or 'No', he had to give a reason or tell me more. Again, I used words to describe what I wanted: 'Tell me more.' 'Tell me why.' 'Explain.'

On other occasions, I'd give him the first question words to help him ask me about the topic: 'I went to the shops today, Jamie.' Pause. 'Ask me "What...?"'

'What are the shops?'

'You mean, "Where are the shops?"'

'Yes.'

'Say it.'

'Where are the shops?'

'I went to the local shops. Ask me another "Wh-" question about my shopping.'

'What did they buy you?'

'Good boy. What did I buy? I bought some shoes for myself.'

After a while, Jamie became very good at using keywords to repeat one word out of my sentence with an upward inflection so that it stood for a question. However, after a while I realised this was the easy away to continue a conversation, so I began to say, 'Not one word. The whole question.' 'Grrr…' he'd say under this breath.

Tip

Make sure your child knows what is expected of them. Give them cue words, half-sentences, obvious directions on how the conversation could develop. Once they've learnt question words, you can supply the cue: 'Give me a "Wh-" question or a "Yes"/"No" question.' In fact you could spend 20 minutes one afternoon going through these different question types and then they'd know how to form questions.

CHAPTER 11

Being an Active Listener for Your Child

Of course we all imagine that we listen to our child, but how closely do we pay attention to their ideas, thoughts and opinions? In my case, Jamie had to repeat his wishes again and again before I took notice of him. It involved the choice of school.

Jamie went to four different schools – three state, one private; two small, two large. In all four, he went to the Special Education sections rather than mainstream classes. We chose the first because it was the closest to us and it was the primary school his sister, Caitlin, went to. He had a difficult time settling into the 'system' of being in a classroom all day and terrified the teacher when he attacked her car because he'd been denied a fishing trip.

The second school was also a state primary with a Special Needs section. Here he started to go to After School Care. This created all kinds of problems. He continually complained of being bullied. He couldn't say that – he only said, 'They hurt me... They angry me.' He got angry over imagined slights and yet the carers assured me the other children were doing nothing more than running past him in their playground games.

By this time, Jamie was about eight or nine and the Special Needs kids regularly joined the mainstream classes for maths and English with the help of their own teacher's aide. I was invited to observe one of these classes and sat at the back while the teacher expounded on isosceles, scalene and right-angled triangles. The teacher stood at the front and drew diagrams on the board while the students copied the work. Jamie looked back at me, his aide tried to interest him in these shapes, and the teacher at the front droned on. If Jamie couldn't understand 'saucepan' or 'flag', what hope did he have of learning and understanding the concept of scalene triangles? I immediately started to look for another school.

By chance, I heard of a local school that specialised in speech and language impairments. It only had about 60 kids in total and the teachers were specialists in occupational therapy or speech and language. Classes were small – fewer than ten – and the grounds were in a restful, rural setting. Although it would mean paying private school fees, it seemed to me the ideal place for Jamie.

After a series of intensive psychological, speech, occupational therapy and intelligence tests, Jamie was accepted. I was thrilled to see him going to a place that would concentrate on developing his conversational skills and one that would not bombard him with concepts and ideas way above his understanding. All went well for a year or so until a new deputy head arrived...

This loud and bombastic woman took control of the school and frequently taught classes. Her ambiguous comments often confused Jamie ('She called us "her uglies". We're not ugly!'). When he had another meltdown, she told him he was a baby, which upset him more.

Also, because the school had no After School Care facilities, Jamie had to go to the local state school down the road, and there he felt even more awkward. The students there were 5–10 years old, yet, by this time, he was 12 going on 13. Again and again, he said to me, 'I'm too old for that place.' But I didn't listen because I didn't want to hear the message. It would have been difficult for me to place him in another school or organise for him to go elsewhere after school. Difficult but not impossible.

He was frequently getting into rages, felt that the younger students were bullying him, disliked this teacher who was taking his classes on a regular basis and resented the After School placement. It was an unhappy time and after one particularly explosive incident, he was suspended from the school.

I was at my wits' end. If a specialist school like this couldn't cope with his needs, what chance did any other school in our city have? I desperately rang the state and private high schools to talk over what they could offer. At one school I was asked, 'Can you son sit in a classroom and take notes from a teacher at the front in subjects like geography, history and social science?' I had to say no. 'Well, that's what we do,' they replied.

Finally, I enrolled him in large state school. It was so big it was called a college and catered for students from pre-school to pre-tertiary, giving it over 1600 students. My soul shrank for Jamie. How would he cope? However, there was some good news. They did have a Special Needs section, called the Enrichment Centre. And Jamie himself was anxious to start once he had visited the campus.

He started in 2009 when he was 15. He spent two and a half years there and never looked back. The maths classes were pre-vocational and contained practical exercises on measurement and personal finances. The English classes were similarly hands-on with projects on taking a holiday, moving out of home, reviewing a film, writing a letter, doing a resume or CV. Communication between me and the teachers was clear and frequent. At least once a week I got an email from one of his teachers, explaining what he needed to do, clarifying how he was doing, asking for advice or giving advice.

Jamie graduated from school in 2011 and won the 'With all my might' award for outstanding effort. More than that, he had gathered over 200 Facebook friends and danced the night away at the Graduation Ball. He loved his time at the college and says it was his best school.

So what can be learnt from this? The only school I really researched turned out to be too constricting and limiting. I thought Jamie could never last in a mainstream school, yet he excelled there. There was no bullying – or even perceived bullying – and the teachers were compassionate and dedicated. I think I learnt two things from the process:

1. Listen to your child and their responses to the learning system.

2. Do not underestimate what your child can cope with.

You can learn as much from your child about the school as you can from prospectuses and meetings with the headteacher. Just listen.

Tips

Small schools may seem ideal, but they are restricted in what they can offer in terms of potential friends. Take a look at larger state schools, especially if they have an excellent Special Needs section embedded in them.

Ask about the communication between teachers and parents: Do the teachers have an email? Do they welcome communication from the parents?

Most important of all, listen to your child's responses to their schooling. What can they cope with? What do they enjoy? What would make their school days happier?

CHAPTER 12

Teaching the Importance of Staying on Topic (Without Over-Indulging in Special Interests)

I once met a man of about 25 who lived in the bush and was a volunteer firefighter. We were at a pub and this man began to talk about firefighting: How often he'd been called out. Which sides of the mountain they'd backburnt. How long the hours were. Who was in charge of operations…on and on and on. He barely looked at me, yet continued to talk to me. Or more precisely, *at* me.

I guessed he must have Asperger's, but it was one of those uncomfortable conversations where I couldn't contribute yet couldn't extricate myself. I just stood there, holding my drink, smiling and nodding, thinking to myself, 'I wonder if I should say to him, "Would you like to ask me a question?"'

Many children with Asperger syndrome have obsessions – trains, dinosaurs, plane crashes – and continue to talk about their topic beyond what is 'normal'. They continue talking (or sometimes asking questions) about their pet topic and frankly it gets boring to the listener. This is staying on topic to the extreme – a topic chosen and pursued relentlessly by one person.

With Jamie, the topic is film. He'll talk about movies all the time. Granted, he will ask you questions about movies, but the topic is always limited to his chosen area. However, there are two or three strategies you can use to divert the conversation.

First, you can use your facial expression to communicate. You can say, 'Look at my face, Jamie. Do I look interested in Wesley Snipes?' You can point to your face in different expressions: 'Here's an interested face – my eyes are wide, my lips are smiling. I'm interested in what you are saying.' And, 'Here's a bored face – my eyes are small, my lips are down. I'm not interested in what you are saying.'

Then you should consider cues to help your child get the conversation on a different tack: 'Do you remember when we saw that film?' or 'Why do you like Wesley Snipes so much?' (Jamie usually said, 'Because he's black' to this.) Or, finally, 'Let's start another conversation. Let's talk about X.'

The Simpsons has always been a favourite of Jamie's. One day he started talking about it and I was getting sick of it. I thought if I heard one more statement about *The Simpsons*, I'd throw the television at the wall. Suddenly, instead of keeping quiet about how I felt, I realised how important it was for Jamie to be aware of his audience.

'Jamie, you haven't asked me if I'm interested in *The Simpsons Halloween Video*. Do you think I'm interested? I'm looking at my computer screen. I'm not watching you while you're talking. I'm not very interested.'

'Oh.'

'Would you like to talk about *The Simpsons*?'

'Yes.'

'Then say, "Can I tell you about *The Simpsons*, mum?" Go on. Ask me.'

'Can I tell you about *The Simpsons*, mum?'

'Yes, you can.'

Make your child realise that not all conversations are acceptable – sometimes you have your own needs in a conversation. Make this clear by signposting it clearly: 'I don't really want to talk about Y today. Why don't you tell me about you. What do you want to do this afternoon?'

Tip

Make sure that your child doesn't turn the conversation to their own special topic and get stuck on that subject. Alert them to the fact that not everyone is interested. Ask them if their ideas follow on from what the speaker said before. Make sure they don't get caught in the trap of self-indulgence.

CHAPTER 13

What is Phatic Communication and Why is it Important?

Good communicators start conversations with strangers or even close friends by using social openers. These can be statements about the weather, asking how a person is, commenting on their dress or jewellery or shaking hands. All these openers of small talk lead the way forward to more significant exchanges. These openers are called phatic communication – the kind of communication when you're not having a conversation.

Jamie has always been bad at this. He finds it difficult to say anything that can be construed as small talk. If he wants to talk at all, it's to launch into a description of a film – its length, director, category and so on, but usually he just stays silent.

So, when we were due to meet two out-of-town relatives at his grandparents and I knew their names, I 'prepped' him. Prepping consists of practising dialogues beforehand. They can be called role-plays, but it's usually just me doing the talking.

'You're going to meet Aunt Velma and Uncle Jo today at grandma and grandad's. You know what would be really nice? If you could say, "How are you today, Aunt Velma?" Or you could say, "Did you come far?" Or, "How long are you staying here?"'

I went through a few options and suggested different things they might say to him. They might ask him about school, so I asked him what he'd reply. When we arrived at the house, Jamie went straight in and said, 'Are you well? I'm very good.' I was so pleased.

Another day we were due to meet some of Jamie's friends at the cinema. I asked him what he was going to talk about.

'I don't know,' he replied.

'Well, you can ask people what they've been doing today.'

'What if they don't know?'

'They should know what they've done.'

'I'll see.'

I wasn't put off. We practised conversation openers again and again and I always praised Jamie after he'd tried. And I always reminded him of the names of the people he was going to be speaking to and asked him to use that person's name in conversation.

Since then, Jamie has learnt a few well-worn openers, like 'How's your work?' and 'How are you going?' Although it's difficult for him to sustain a longer conversation based around these openers, at least it makes him fit in with others and they don't realise his difficulty using phatic communication.

Tips

The Child Development Institute of California states on its website that at six months a typical child will be 'aware of the social value of speech'. Jamie has never been aware of that – not at six months nor at six years. He is slowly becoming aware that he has responsibilities in any conversation but we are a long way from his being able to deliver on those responsibilities. He is, however, at the first level – he knows that something is required of him. That is the first stage that you have to bring your child to.

Practise conversations you can predict with some certainty. And congratulate your child afterwards with whatever they come out with.

Debrief any difficulties or strange requests, explaining what the person was asking and how your child could have answered.

CHAPTER 14

Encouraging the Use of Names

In all discussions of active listening (and sales pitches), we are told 'there is no sound more beautiful to anyone than their own name', and even if it's not an essential, it certainly is a good stepping-stone to getting on with others. It's why we have name badges and 'getting-to-know-you' exercises at the beginning of workshops.

But this has been one of the most difficult concepts for Jamie to grasp. For a long time, I tried to get Jamie to use and learn people's names in conversation. It's one of those lessons he finds very difficult as he either forgets the name immediately or can't place the face. However, in the beginning I tried very basic methods.

First of all, I would forewarn Jamie if we were going over to someone's place and remind him of the names of the hosts. Then I'd practise with him by saying, 'You're going to meet John and Carla so when you see them, you'll say "Hello, John" and "Hi, Carla". This will make them feel good.' I'd then get him to repeat the phrases after me.

Later when he had interviews (with respite carers, service deliverers and later at job interviews), I'd say beforehand, 'You're going to have an interview and you have to mention the interviewer's name. Can you think how to use it?' Jamie would usually need some nudging to say, 'How are you, Sally?' and so on, but after the interviews I attended, we'd debrief ('Did you make eye contact/use her name/not fidget/etcetera?'). And using the person's name was always his weakness.

Then one day we got the school newsletter in hard copy. I looked at the photos and recognised some of his classmates.

'Who's this?' I asked.

'That's Nicholas,' he replied.

'And what's his surname?'

'Cerebos.'

'So you know his name? That's good. Now when you see him, remember to use his name. Okay?'

'Okay.'

The photos in the newsletter consolidated Jamie's knowledge and by working out some role-plays, I could make sure he used his friends' names. This expanded in later years, when his secondary school brought out a Year Book at the end of the academic year. He sought out faces he could add as friends on his Facebook and I reminded him to use their names when he was with them so that he could show he was listening to them and being polite.

Tips

Use photos in the school newsletter to practise names. Ask: 'Who's that?' 'What's this girl's name?' and 'Do they use your name when they speak to you?' You can also use class photos with the names of students underneath to help your child 'find' their friends and name them.

Year Books are also very useful as you get a list of names and faces. You can extend the conversation to 'Do you know X?' or 'Is Y in your class?' or 'Look, here's X. He's playing football. Do you play football with him?'

CHAPTER 15

How to Help Family and Friends Have Conversations with Your Child

How to get others to talk to your child... Of course, the problem is not getting other people – friends and family – to talk to your child. They do. All the time. But the conversations are usually one-sided:

Aunt: 'And did you have a good day?'

Child: 'Yes.'

Aunt: 'Do you like your school?'

Child: 'Yes.'

Aunt: 'Did you get my present?'

Child: 'No.'

Come to think of it, conversations with teenagers usually run along these tracks anyway...

However, with our children these conversations occur all too often and it's difficult to role-play the 'correct' or 'better' way to relate to friends and family. So the method to follow is to 'coach' the adults directly.

At first I asked my friends to do as I did: ask 'Wh-' questions: '*Where* did you go?', '*What* did you do?' and so on. However, Jamie answered again in monosyllables, even if he did in fact know the answer ('Shops', 'Swimming' and so on). Therefore, these questions became conversation stoppers instead of openers.

I happened across a better approach one day when we were talking about his soccer game. I knew that he had had one because Physical Education was on the timetable. After a few attempts to extract information ('It was hot', 'We won' and so on), I said:

'Tell me about the game.'

Jamie paused for a long while. I thought he wasn't going to say anything and then he said, 'Annie got hurt.'

'Really?'

'Yes.'

'Tell me more about it.'

'She fell.'

'Oh. Did she trip? Did she fall over something?'

'Yes.'

'Did she stay on the field? Or did she go off?'

'She...er...went off.'

I then repeated what he had told me as a story: 'So you played soccer today and Annie had an accident. She tripped and fell and she was hurt so she went off the field.'

I turned to Jamie who was smiling as if he'd said all that. 'Go on,' I encouraged. 'You say it. Tell me the story.'

And he did. That was the first time I heard Jamie tell me a story.

I suddenly realised that the opening 'Tell me about...' or 'Tell me more about...' was a powerful yet simple tool. The other questions ('Where...?', 'What...?', 'Why...?') direct and supply their own answers, but 'Tell me about...' allows children to supply as much or as little as they like. It can stimulate conversation in any number of different directions and it is led by the person who answers.

So I then started telling friends and family to use this conversational opener, but I also warned them that Jamie was likely to say nothing at first and that they should give him time to formulate something. This then allowed many simple conversations to take place and for the adults to learn something about my son.

Tips

Explain to your friends and family that the best way to get your child to talk is to use an open-ended statement like:

'Tell me about...'

'I'd like to know more about...'

'Tell me more.'

They can then follow up with further questions and at the end, summarise the complete 'story' as a whole. This will help your child build narratives of their own life and consolidate their memory of events.

Alert your family and friends that it may take some time before your child can assemble thoughts for an answer, but that they should wait attentively and eventually, your child will say something.

When you get home you can ask your child to write down these sentences in a 'diary'. It can – and should be – very short, but it will serve as a good prompt for reflection in the future and also a measure of their progress over time.

CHAPTER 16

Talking About Body Language and Emotions with Your Child

As we grow up, we instinctively learn the features of body language – how someone looks when they're angry, how they stand when they're insecure, how their eyelashes flutter when they're lying. And yet this instinctive knowledge seems denied to our children on the autistic spectrum. Generally, they find it difficult to interpret different body cues, and many of these children don't display any of them themselves at all.

Surprisingly, Jamie has always been emotive in his expressions and body language, but he still had difficulty in interpreting these signs in others, so I made a point of 'interpreting' them for him. The first place I started was in films. As we would watch videos and DVDs together, I'd put names to emotions: 'You can see he's upset now, can't you?' 'She's really frightened, isn't she?' 'I think he's bored.'

After naming the emotion, I'd describe the body language: 'You can tell he's worried because he's got wrinkles on his forehead.' 'You can see she's frightened because she's trembling.'

This seemed to be particularly successful with cartoons and I'd do the action for him to show what I meant (as the words alone often meant nothing). Then, once I'd named the emotion, described the body language and demonstrated it, I'd ask him how someone acts when they're feeling that emotion: 'You're Buzz Lightyear and you're very angry. What do you do?' 'You're Dumbo and you're scared. What do you look like?'

Jamie quite enjoyed playing these pretend games, never realising they were consolidating his knowledge of body language. He'd act each one out and giggle as I made a bigger fuss of the expressions or the body twisting and shaking. It was a great game.

Later on, I'd take advantage of every opportunity to describe his own actions and expressions to him again. I remember one time when I went to collect him from a birthday party only to find him sitting dejectedly on the sofa. The other kids were playing and laughing, but Jamie was alone. He didn't look up when I came in. I walked over to him and kneeled down to him, facing him directly.

'I can see from your body language you're upset. Your shoulders are down. Your eyes are looking at the floor. You aren't looking at me. Am I right?'

'Yes.'

'So what's wrong?'

And, in his stumbling, incoherent way he told me what was the matter.

We need to have a language to describe non-verbals, and the more often we use, interpret and describe fictional characters', our own and our child's body language, we are giving our children a key to understanding their own and other people's natures.

When Jamie was young, his emotions often spilled over and erupted into rages of frustration and disappointment. It was frightening to watch and made me feel so impotent. I can remember times when he punched his fist through the kitchen wall, when he kicked the teacher's car door in, when he fouled up the pipes with stones he pelted at the plumbing. There never seemed to be a day that went by without some crisis in our lives.

The first clue I had to help me with these fits came from a speech pathologist who listened to me when I talked about Jamie's 'tantrums'. Jamie was about six at the time and I was explaining how Jamie would suddenly fly off into a rage. She said that the emotion of anger was the most difficult to control for people with autism or Asperger's and one way she had found to moderate it was to use a visual gauge of the emotion and ask the child to 'rate' themselves on it.

She pulled out a laminated card with a thermometer gauge drawn on it. The thermometer had markings 0–10 on the side and she asked Jamie how he had felt when he threw the plate of food on the floor.

'Were you very, very angry?... A ten?... Or were you not so angry?... A six?'

He pointed to the ten.

'I see,' she said, colouring in the gauge to the top. 'So you were really, really angry.'

He nodded.

'Then you can take this and put it on your fridge and when you get angry, you can say how angry you are.'

I don't know whether it worked because Jamie has an affinity with numbers or whether it was because it was a visual instead of some indefinable feeling, but that thermometer came in very useful in the moments of high passion that occurred in our home. He'd start to get angry, going red in the face and panting quickly, and I'd just say, 'I can see you're angry. Your face is going red. You're breathing fast. Come to the fridge. Let's look at the thermometer. Talk to me. Tell me how many.' It didn't work instantaneously, but it distracted him so that his attention went elsewhere.

The very fact of naming his emotion seemed to calm him down; at least, it made the experience more objective. And when I started to think about the benefits of this strategy, I realised that I could do the same with other emotions. When he was scared by a small puppy, I asked him how scared he was and, although he was nervous, he'd reply with a number.

The judgement of how extensive the feeling was seemed to calm him and help him move to a kind of equilibrium.

With the aid of such pantomime, games, videos and the 'thermometer', it became easier to talk about Jamie's moods (which were sometimes extreme) and, ultimately, to help him control them. More than that, they helped him explore the silent world of gestures and expressions.

Tips

Use characters in films to 'decode' simple body language for your child.

Talk about the characters' feelings and afterwards mimic their expressions and gestures to show your child how that feeling is expressed.

Find your local distributor of software and hardware for people with disabilities. Look up programmes for people with autism that concentrate on decoding emotions and expressions.

However often your child erupts, take them through the steps of calming, describing, explaining, defusing and then debriefing.

Consolidate your child's knowledge of body language by describing your understanding of their actions and expressions *as they happen*. You will never get a better chance to help them understand body language in action.

CHAPTER 17

Understanding the Importance of Pauses and Silence

So far in this book, I have stressed the ways in which you can engage your child in conversation and this has involved you talking to them, explaining situations and the game of conversation. It may seem odd but now I want to talk about how important pauses and silence are in a conversation with your child.

You don't always have to speak to get a message across or to get your child to speak.

There are two key situations where you will find that pauses and silence will help your child much more than words:

1. You allow a space to exist and your child realises they have to fill it to complete the conversation.

2. Your child is so full of emotion that words will only come between you.

Let me give you a couple of examples:

First, in social situations you will often want to intervene to model the correct way for your child to interact with a peer. And you're likely to interrupt with language and thereby take over. When Jamie met anyone for the first time, I would intervene and start talking, using Jamie's words: 'Hi, Peter, it's nice to meet you.'

It only took a few attempts at this for me to realise that Jamie hated this approach. He started to scowl at me and seethe, whispering, 'I know... I know!' through clenched teeth.

A much more successful way was to practise the role-play beforehand, saying, 'Now when you meet Peter, what will you say?... And what else could you ask him?'

Another type of interaction was the conversation between the two of us, which I tried to make as natural as possible. When I started working on conversational therapy, I was so keen to squeeze the most out of each conversation that I would guide Jamie through all the possible answers he could give me:

'Shall we go to the cinema?'

'Hmm... Er... I...er...'

'You can say, "Yes, I'd like to go and see this." Or you can say, "No, thanks, mum, I'd rather do that."'

This all got too much for Jamie – working out whose words I was saying, trying to guess what he was supposed to say, making it difficult for him to know how to answer. Much later, I realised that it was better for me to simply ask the question and let him find his own words. Modelling all the time only complicated the issue.

In these examples I was trying too hard to help him along the way and he, rather naturally, got irritated. But on other occasions, it became an actual obstacle to Jamie's emotional balance. There was the time Jamie ran to me totally frustrated with his sister. Outraged and angry, he spluttered and coughed and tears streamed down his face. Straightaway I tried to find out what had happened.

I asked him questions. I made suggestions. I tried to reconstruct events from his broken words. All the time that I was asking him about the incident, he was getting more and more upset and I realised that what he wanted wasn't questions, it was comfort.

If I had held my arms open to him, nodded in sympathetic agreement, got myself down to his level and held him close, I would have really comforted him. Silence and non-verbals are far more powerful pacifiers than words. And after that, I tried to shut my mouth and think of what I would like in that situation.

Tips

Try not to 'over-talk'. Words are a problem for our children. Even more words confuse them.

Leave pauses between your questions and your child's answers so that they have time to consider their responses.

When your child is emotional, don't leap in with sentences, advice, questions or comments. Just close your mouth and open your arms.

CHAPTER 18

Making the Most of Stories and Story-Telling

We all love stories – we need them in our lives. They entertain us, teach us right from wrong, help us understand character and provide imagery, but they also give structure to our own personal histories. Throughout our lives we work and rework the different coloured threads of our narrative to reflect on what's past and to conjure up our futures. Our children are different. They find it difficult to tell stories, but you can use the stories around them – in film, TV and books – to create a larger world for them and lead them into their own re-creation of their lives.

The first place every modern parent goes nowadays to entertain their child is the DVD player, and cartoons are likely to be the first images our children see. The personalities of Bambi, Asterix, Buzz Lightyear and Shrek are the earliest strangers our children encounter. And they can relive their stories again and again.

Once I realised the importance of stories, I sat down and watched these films with my son. I put the subtitles on so that Jamie could see what was being said and subliminally learn to recognise word shapes over continued watching. I held the remote and stopped the film to explain what people were saying or what particular words meant. I did pantomimes of the characters' facial expressions. I then recapped the film every so often by asking Jamie what had happened (with specific questions) and at the end I re-told the story to him, maybe days later.

This had several benefits – it enlarged his very poor vocabulary, it helped him learn to recognise facial expressions, it gave him a sense of achievement when he could answer my questions and in the end he could relate the whole story to me. We had many pleasant car trips piecing together these animated fables.

But there are also books. Ever since Jamie was young, I had read to him each night. When he moved to a new school at the age of ten, I 'admitted' to the teacher that I still read to him. She encouraged me, saying she wished more parents continued the tradition. In the beginning it was the cartoon stories of the Powerpuff girls and the beautiful stories by Mem Fox, but later he started to choose his own and felt a great affinity for the Tintin books. I don't know why these detailed and intricate stories of opium sales, smuggling, kidnapping and political upheaval attracted him, but they did.

Jamie has never enjoyed reading to himself, but he loved those bedtime stories and when, years later, he became interested in the James Bond films and I found him on Wiki poring over the list of the titles in the series, I invited him to make a 'James Bond' book himself. He was about 14 and we got a simple exercise book, covered it with some gift wrapping, put a sticky label on it, saying 'The James Bond Book' and Jamie faithfully copied all the titles in a table, saying when they'd been made, who starred in them and how much they grossed. He then wrote down the titles of the theme songs and printed and cut out pictures of the movie stills.

All of this involved researching, selecting, printing, pasting, illustrating and talking about his choices. It also gave him a project to be proud of. The next time a friend came over for dinner, Jamie pulled out the exercise book (rather nonchalantly) and pushed it across the table to show the visitor. He wanted to share his achievement and talk about his pet topic.

James Bond
1. 1962 Dr. No
2. 1963 From Russia with Love
3. 1964 Goldfinger
4. 1965 Thunderball
5. 1967 You only Live Twice
6. 1969 On Her Majesty's Secret Service
7. 1971 Diamonds are forever
8. 1973 Live and let die
9. 1974 The man with the Golden Gun
10. 1977 The Spy who Loved me
11. 1979 Moonraker
12. 1981 for your eyes only
13. 1983 Octopussy
14. 1985 A view to Kill
15. 1987 The Living daylights
16. 1989 Licence to Kill
17. 1995 Goldeneye
18. 1997 Tomorrow never dies
19. 1999 The World is not enough
20. 2002 die Another day
21. 2006 Casino royale
22. 2008 Quantum of Solace

Finally, when I'd got Jamie talking about his films, I started on his days. I'd ask him to tell me three things about his day and wove them into a coherent whole. In the evening – just sometimes – I'd suggest he write them in a book we called his diary. Just two or three sentences, but it helped him piece his life together.

Baby steps, baby steps…

Tips

Let your child guide their reading. Take them to book shops and libraries regularly and let them choose their own stories. Whatever these stories are, they open up a world of colour and exploration. Make it a treat.

Spend time with your child watching their favourite videos. Use the pause button to explain or comment on the story.

Expand their vocabulary and get them actively involved in the dialogue, sets, costumes, quotes and so on.

Make a fun project of anything your child is interested in. It can be dinosaurs, trains, honey-bees or trucks. There'll be plenty on the internet and they can create their own book. Then you can encourage them to share it with visitors and talk about it.

CHAPTER 19

Using Mind-Maps to Improve Conversation

While I was thinking about stories and their importance in language learning, I realised that I could use mind-maps to help expand Jamie's vocabulary.

Mind-maps are idea generators and I often use them in my textbook writing. They are a valuable tool in thought showering and are easy to create. You start off with a large piece of paper and write the subject of your thoughts in the middle of the page in a circle. You then think of all related ideas and draw arrows and circles to new ideas. The best way to generate ideas is to think of the answers to the 'Who?', 'What?', 'When?', 'Where?', 'Why?' and 'How?' questions (e.g. 'Who will do it?', 'Who is affected?', 'Who was there?' etc.).

I bought a large scrapbook and some coloured pens and sat Jamie down quietly at the dining table.

'Okay, we're going to play a game now.' He looked happy.

'With pens?'

'Yes. We're going to talk about what we did at the weekend.'

'The weekend?'

'Yes, you remember. Saturday and Sunday. Where did we go?'

'Ermmm… Skating?'

'Yes, that's right.' And I wrote 'WEEKEND' in a large circle in the centre of the page. Then I drew a line from it to another circle, in which I wrote 'SKATING'. 'What did we wear?'

'Er… Boots?'

'Yes, those boots are called "ice-skates".' And I wrote down 'ice-skates' in a smaller circle. 'And where was the ice rink?'

'In Australia?'

'Yes, it's in Brisbane. We live in Brisbane.' So I wrote 'Brisbane' in another circle off the skating circle.

We continued until we had filled the page with our activities. I was doing the writing and correcting of language and Jamie was seeing it come to life on the page.

'Now I think we've got some pictures of our trip to the market and the skating rink. Shall we print them off and put them in the right place on the map?'

'Oh, yes!'

So we printed off some photos – Jamie chose them – and I was careful to include as many different language items as possible: 'Here you are, putting your socks on.' 'The floor is red, isn't it?' 'That ice-cream was cold, wasn't it?' And so on.

At the end we glued the photos to the mind-map showing our weekend and the next time visitors came round, Jamie proudly showed them his work.

Tip

I can't praise mind-maps enough – they let your child learn the written language without realising it, they encourage natural speech, they let the child generate their own answers and they stimulate closeness on a shared project.

You can also use mind-maps to encourage your child to tell you about a birthday party they just attended, a trip to the beach, a film they saw, a book they had read to them, someone they met. And you don't need to restrict it to words. These mind-maps can be illustrated by you and your child and then displayed on a notice-board. You can add cut-outs of theatre programmes, bus tickets, postcards, photos or anything that relates to the subject. If you keep these mind-maps in a scrapbook, you can go back and spend time re-reading them later and reinforcing the language/vocabulary/structures used.

CHAPTER 20

Coping with Idioms and Incorrect English

Jamie has always had problems forming correct language patterns. At one stage, he was always saying 'look' for 'sound', as in 'This music looks good'. At another stage he prefaced everything he said with 'Besides…', as in 'Besides me I don't like peanuts'. Then, of course, there were all the common grammatical mistakes that all children make with their language – for example: 'I bcen to the cinema.' 'Do you be happy?'

At the same time, there were many features of language he just didn't understand, such as idioms. Idioms are groups of words that have a meaning that's not obvious from the individual words. For example, 'It's raining cats and dogs', 'Have a chip on your shoulder', 'You're barking up the wrong tree', and so on. Jamie was constantly confused by these expressions, so I had to keep on explaining them to him.

Jamie needed help with both these aspects of language learning and language comprehension.

To address the first, that of incorrect language, I made sure that I supplied the correct version for him. I didn't tell him he was wrong but instead said, 'We don't usually say that. We usually say, "I've been to the cinema" or "Are you happy?"' Apparently, most parents rarely correct their children's mother tongue, and the kids usually pick up on their mistakes later. But Jamie needed extra help so I went out of my way to supply the correct version. This, of course, didn't correct the problem immediately, but it did show him that there was a 'standard' way of speaking.

The other problem, that of understanding idioms, was more difficult to address because there are so many of them in English. And there are not only idioms that don't make sense at first sight; there are also phrasal verbs (a verb plus preposition or adverb which has a different meaning, such as: 'to make up', 'to put someone down', 'to cook up an excuse'); proverbs ('a bird in the hand is worth two in the bush'); and collocations ('a blonde woman' but not a 'blonde car'; 'a rising star' but not 'a lifting/climbing star').

As Jamie was attending a specialist school for speech- and language-impaired children at the time, they did lay particular emphasis on idioms and other tricky expressions and sent Jamie home with pictures of idioms – a cartoon of a cup of tea and a child shaking his head ('It's not his cup of tea'), but it was a mammoth task to teach the thousands of idioms individually.

I found a different way of talking to Jamie about them. When they came up in conversation naturally, I used the word 'idiom' (whatever kind of expression they were that presented problems). Although I thought Jamie would never be able to understand what the word 'idiom' meant – after all, many native speakers don't know – I knew he would come to recognise the word as meaning 'this is a tricky bit of language'. And he did. Later, whenever he came across something he didn't understand, he'd say, 'That's an idiom, isn't it?' and then I could take the opportunity to explain it to him. 'Idiom' became a catchword for anything that didn't make sense.

One day we were out walking the dog and we came to a viewing spot. 'Isn't this beautiful?' I said to Jamie. 'Now you say something.'

'I think Odin likes it,' he said after a minute or two. We looked down at Odin, who promptly pooped on the ground. 'I think that's the icing on the cake,' said Jamie proudly. 'That's an idiom, isn't it?'

Tips

Try to correct any mistakes in your child's grammar by saying, 'We don't usually say that. We say this…' That way they won't feel they're constantly getting things wrong.

Teach your child the term 'idiom' as something that doesn't make sense immediately. You can use the term loosely to describe any expression they can't understand. Once you have a term to describe these odd phrases, you can explain the particulars and your child will learn to understand their meaning. Also, if you can, try to reuse particular idioms you've explained to your child before.

CHAPTER 21

Teaching Your Child to Verbalise Distress (and Avoid a Meltdown)

Ever since we had embarked on the Points System – see Chapter 6 – I had a gauge for Jamie to measure his behaviour. It proved invaluable. Jamie always started the day with 10/10 and could often earn more than that if he was especially good.

I was pleased he had taken to a methodical system like that, rather than my leaning on extra helpings of food or expensive trips out to encourage him, but the greatest modifier of all is really my attitude to him. He cares so much about what I think of him.

Let me give you an example: His sister Skyped me in despair one night. She had just come from an Easter dinner with her grandparents where Jamie had 'thrown a tantrum' and punched the fridge. She didn't think she'd done anything to start it, but now he was getting big (at aged 17 he stood 6 feet tall and weighed 12½ stone) and she was fearful for herself and the family. She calmed down while she spoke and we talked about how we could possibly explain to Jamie the difference between being angry – which everyone does at some time – and violent outbursts which are downright dangerous.

I sat at home and waited for him to come back, and as I waited, I thought of what I would say. I decided on four things:

1.   I would find out what had started it all (catalyst).

2. I would tell him he couldn't hurt other people (reprimand).

3. I would stop him using the Xbox for four days (consequence).

4. He would have to apologise to Caitlin *and explain to her the reason he got so angry* before he could have another driving lesson – a real treat at that stage (verbalising his apology).

He came in looking sullen and watchful. I asked him what had happened. He eyed me suspiciously, saying, 'You heard?' (He must think, like Hogwarts, we have flocks of owls sending instantaneous messages back and forth between family members.)

I said I had heard and asked him to explain to me his feelings. He told me in simple sentences that Caitlin had asked him to phone Grandad from the airport but Jamie hadn't got his mobile with him so he couldn't use it. The story behind why he hadn't got his phone was a complicated one and he was utterly confused. He thought he was being asked to do something he couldn't.

'She kept blocking me,' he said.

'Blocking? You mean, like standing in front of you?'

'No, saying something. All the time she was saying something.'

'Ah, that's interrupting. She was *interrupting* you.'

'Yes.'

I told him straightaway that I was glad he had spoken so clearly and explained the problem to me. I reassured him that Caitlin often spoke quickly because she was very clever and it was difficult to find the right words to answer her. Therefore, I told him, whenever someone said something that was difficult for him to reply to (his mobile was at home charging), he should say, 'Please stop talking. I can't think.' I repeated that a few times during our conversation so that he had it in his head as a mantra that hopefully he would use in the future.

Then I went on to explain the consequences of his outburst. 'Sometimes we get angry. We all get angry at some things. But there is good anger and bad anger. Good anger is explaining why we're angry or taking time out like you did two weeks ago' – we'd had another 'situation' when Jamie had walked away from a highly volatile scene – 'and bad anger is where you hit someone or something.' I paused. 'You can *never, never, never* have bad anger. If you do, you will go to court and you will go to prison.'

His eyes widened. I didn't need to repeat myself.

'*I* will report you and *I* will send you to court. Do you know why you can't have bad anger?'

'Because I'm a man.' He started to cry.

'Yes. You're a big, strong man and you frighten people around you and you might hurt them. That's dangerous.' I didn't need to say any more about the reprimand. 'Therefore, I have to think of a punishment. And so you will not play on the Xbox for four days.' I didn't need to repeat the consequences. 'But people need to know *why* you get bad anger. I know it's difficult. Particularly for you. You are an Aspie and you have difficulty with language. But you told me, just now. You told me clearly. So I want you to tell Caitlin when you apologise to her. It may not be today. It may not be next week. But before we can be a family again, you will say you're sorry and explain why you got upset. And you won't have a driving lesson until you do.'

That was enough. He had remained quiet throughout my assessment and judgement of the situation. Now I wanted to encourage him.

'But,' I said with a smile on my face, 'I know you can do it. I know you can. Do you remember when I told you that Aspies were sensitive to noise and that's why you didn't like Caitlin humming or Nana playing the piano? And after that, you came to me and said you were going to let them do those things because it made them happy?'

'Yes?'

'That was four months ago and you've never stopped me playing my radio since. I've been watching you and you have worked on your feelings for noise. I have faith in you. Becca has faith in you. Caitie has faith in you. We believe you can change – something so many people cannot do. They can't change themselves. But you actually work on yourself – you work to make yourself a better person. You think, "How can I do this better?" And you will work on your bad anger – and I will help you. You have tremendous power and you can do good.'

That was the encourager.

Tip

These are particularly fraught times when tempers are high. In this case, I had the benefit of being away from the explosion. If I'd been there, I'm sure I would have blamed Caitlin and, because I know it's not good to talk to Jamie in those moods, she would have thought I was condoning his behaviour. But I know he needs time and space to distance himself from the situation before he can possibly 'work things out'. Talking and asking him won't help *at the time*.

This scenario also gave me an hour or two to prepare my response and I think the following process is applicable to many turbulent times – *afterwards*:

Work out *why* it happened.

Explain the *consequences*.

Explain the *reprimand* or *punishment*.

Give your child a follow-up *action* – usually an apology. *Encourage* your child.

Sometimes timing is all.

CHAPTER 22

Conversation Starters in the Supermarket

I remember once years ago, watching a TV documentary on a social programme in the United States that sought to improve the literacy of children with single mothers. Part of the programme involved a social worker/educator visiting the families at home and suggesting practical ways the mothers could start educating their children.

The first thing she recommended – and this was for a child of three or four – was that a trip to the supermarket could be a learning experience for the child. As the mother came home and unpacked the groceries, she got the child to help her and they counted out the items together as they put them away. 'One, two, three, four, five apples... One jar of jam... Two tubes of toothpaste...' and so on.

This struck me as having a number of benefits:

1. They're both doing something together, something that's normally a chore for the parent(s) but is now fun. It becomes a game and one that both of them can enjoy.

2. It's teaching by repetition the numbers under ten.

3. It's increasing the child's vocabulary.

This, of course, was being offered to young children, but the same principle can apply to older children or speech- and language-impaired children like Jamie.

My husband, Andrew, had always done the grocery shopping and after he died, I had to take Jamie with me on my trips to the supermarket. At first I avoided it, and went during school hours so that he wasn't involved. But later I remembered this story of the mothers in South Carolina and I started to take him with me as an educational trip.

This must have begun when he was about six. I wheeled the trolley to the right place, then asked him to pull out the six potatoes we needed or the green hair shampoo. At first I began with the foodstuffs he recognised – his yoghurts, the milk we usually got, the butter we used. It was quite a passive role for him. I didn't expect him to speak – just to listen and follow instructions.

After each visit he became more familiar with the products I usually wanted and by the time he was eight, he could run off and get them for me. I always followed behind him as he made his way to the dairy or cereals or whatever he was getting. By the time he was ten, he and his sister were always accompanying me on shopping trips and they became essential helpers. Apart from being a boon in the weekly shop, it also made shopping a game and fun. As Jamie grew more confident around the supermarket and with the items, he eventually went off on his own to collect what we needed.

In recent years, I've stretched Jamie. I've no need to watch him and he knows my route around the supermarket so he knows where he'll find me. In order to extend his abilities, I send him off to find things he hasn't heard of before, such as bleach or cocoa or smoked salmon. (Then, as a treat, I'll pop in 'some mints'.)

'Now we need some breadcrumbs, Jamie,' I'll say.

He looks puzzled and doubtful that we really need anything as obscure as breadcrumbs.

'Breadcrumbs make your fish and vegetables. I put egg white and breadcrumbs on the fish and then fry it. We've run out. So we need some more.'

Jamie still looks at me as if this task is too enormous to contemplate.

'Now what we do first is look at the lists at the end of the aisle.' We go to the laminated list hanging at the end of each aisle. (Luckily, Jamie has been able to read since about the age of seven and recognise an alphabetical order since the age of ten.)

'No "breadcrumbs",' he says.

'Then do you know what we do now?' I ask.

His brow furrows.

'We ask someone who works here.'

He brightens as if this solves the problem.

'Let's go find someone who works here,' I say and head off to find a staff member. First, before we go up to that person, I point out to Jamie how I can tell that the person works in the store – he or she is wearing a uniform. The uniform is a certain colour. That person may be standing behind a counter or coming out of doors that say 'Staff only'. I explain what the words mean and how we can't enter. Then I rehearse or role-play the conversation I want him to have with the staff member.

'You want to find breadcrumbs, so what do you say to that man?'

'Where are the breadcrumbs?'

'That's right, Jamie.'

But before you can send your child off to have a conversation with the staff member, you have to rehearse what that person is likely to say to your child, because your child is not likely to understand or remember what they say.

'Now when you ask him where the breadcrumbs are, he will probably say, "In aisle 5" or "In aisle 2". You have to remember what he says. Do you think you can do that?'

Jamie nods.

'And he may also say, "On the left" or "At the bottom". Can you remember that?'

'I think so.'

'Right, you go off and ask him.'

And you watch with pride as your child goes into the distance to hold a purposeful conversation with a complete stranger and know that he is growing and becoming a citizen of the great world beyond the confines of your little family...

Tips

Use counting and colours as often as you can at the supermarket.

Practise teaching and testing your child on the staple items you buy each week.

Gradually ask your child to go to collect the items for you as you follow behind.

Introduce your child to the signs above each aisle (and introduce the word 'aisle' very quickly) and the laminated lists at the end of each aisle or hanging signboards above if your supermarket has them. Both these aides help your child to practise reading for some purpose and recognising alphabetical orders.

Get your child to take responsibility for sharing the lifting, packing, unloading and putting away of the groceries.

When unpacking at home, use this as an opportunity for practising locations – 'Put the bread in the bread bin... Put the milk in the fridge door...'

Put plenty of time aside for supermarket shopping and make it a leisurely event that allows you quality time with your child.

CHAPTER 23

Conversation Starters on Car Journeys

Everyone has played games in the car at some stage in their lives – just think of I-Spy. For our kids, though, games provide practice in an informal setting not only to improve their observation, memory, reasoning, guesswork and problem-solving, but also to be key tool in conversation.

As Jamie was growing up, I suppose we were typical of middle-class parents and kids around the world – we travelled a lot in the car and it made the ideal location for extended conversations or games. I started very early with Jamie, giving him colour games: 'What can you see that's black?' 'Can you see something green?' And then spelling games: 'What begins with B?' 'How many letters in "cat"?' 'What letter ends the word "seat"?' This supplemented his alphabet learning and, of course, when he got any answer right, it was his turn to ask me.

We also played 'registration plates', which involves reading the letters in a registration plate and making up nonsense sentences, for example, 'RGB... Hmmm... Right Good Boy' or 'SFQ... Safety First Queen'. It may seem strange that we played word games with a boy who had severe speech problems, but Jamie responded well to them and enjoyed playing them.

When we were travelling through a country area, we counted the number of farm animals we could see or we'd just count sheep. When we were travelling in England, we'd shout if we saw a pub sign with legs, for example, 'The Pig and Boy' would equal four points for the four legs of the pig and two points for the two legs of the boy. This was a game we played with Jamie's older sister and it took some time for Jamie to get the hang of it, but after a while it made sense to him.

Later on, when Jamie was older, he could take part in a modified game 'Categories' (or B for Botticelli) where you have to think of an item/person beginning with a certain letter of the alphabet and belonging to a category, for example, 'Apple for A; Banana for B; Carrot for C' when you're looking for fruit and vegetables. With Jamie I asked him to think of as many items/people with the same initial letter – they didn't have to belong to a category. (The best letters are B, C, P, S, R and T.)

We also played maths games related to whatever he was doing in maths class at the time. Jamie was absolutely entranced by the idea of Roman numerals when he was nine. I think it was because he thought it was a code. Anyway, as soon as I picked up on his interest, I started asking him to 'translate': 'What's VII?' 'What's IX?' and so on up to the higher combinations like 'MCVVII'. Then we started from Arabic to Roman: 'What's 42?' He loved it. He loved being good at something when so much schooling was a chore.

Later we moved to fractions. That was more difficult without pen and paper but I started off with fractions that add up to one: two halves, three thirds, seven sevenths, sixteen sixteenths. Once he had this concept, I gave him simple additions: one half plus one half; two thirds plus three thirds. And again he asked me questions after I'd asked him questions.

Generally, I let his schooling guide as to games – whatever stage he was at was where I started. Sometimes he didn't want to play, but usually – particularly where points were to be won – he took to it.

Tips

Find out what your child is learning at the moment in class and invent some games for the car.

Use your child's own interests to lead you in any way they like – for example, they might be fascinated by cars so you could invent an I-Spy for car brands; or if they are interested in dogs, you could play a 'spot the dachshund/etc.' game.

Don't push your child if they lose interest or find it too difficult. Keep it fun.

CHAPTER 24

Conversation Starters and Special Interests

It was the middle of the holidays. I'd been taking Jamie to the gym and organising trips to the beach, but we'd (I'd) run out of ideas of things to do. Jamie was playing on his computer – his default activity when nothing was planned, then he turned to me and said, 'Why is he "Dr. No"? Is he a doctor who says, "No"?' I realised he was looking up information on James Bond films.

Lately, he'd become interested in James Bond. I think it was mainly because the films form a series and Jamie loves groups of objects. (He is the devotee of the collective noun.) Anyway, he had seen *Quantum of Solace* a couple of times and after that, he wanted to see the earlier Bond films. But he had to start at the beginning so we had been to Wikipedia to find out their order. Now he was checking them out.

I made the whole process of finding the Bond films into a game, with Jamie looking up James Bond on Google, finding the list of hits, and me directing him to follow up the Wiki entry. Up came a comprehensive list in order with the title, actor, director, gross sales, budget and total sales in current dollar value. This required some explanation from me but Jamie was fired up.

I suddenly realised how interested he was in this task. Catching his enthusiasm, I said, 'You should be grateful to your school and your teachers that you know how to read all this information.' (He'd been complaining about school on and off, saying the teachers made him work.)

Then it suddenly struck me – why not make a project of James Bond? 'Jamie – would you like to make a book on James Bond?'

His face lit up. 'Sure!'

So we set about making a book. First I got an old exercise book, tore out the pages with my writing on and went to my collection of gift paper. I asked Jamie to choose a sheet to cover his book. He chose a *Pirates of the Caribbean* piece. He and I both covered the book and he learnt how to measure the sheet correctly, fold, cut and sticky-tape the edges. Then I asked him to get some white stickers and write the name of the book and his name on two different stickers. That done, he proudly stuck the stickers to the front cover and held it up for me.

Then we went back to Wiki. He copied out the list of the films in order, together with their year of production. I helped him brighten the page with different coloured inks.

As he was involved in the list, he asked some strange, but typical, questions, like, 'Is Octopussy an octopus and a pussy?' and 'Is Russia in love with someone?' I praised these questions, telling him these were funny, interesting questions that no-one had asked before. Then I realised how true it was. These questions were Jamie's view on James Bond.

Quickly I printed off a photo of Jamie and asked him to cut it out. Then I asked him to glue it to the centre of the next page in his James Bond book and write his questions down. I helped him draw speech bubbles around the questions and a cute page appeared before us.

I asked him whether he'd like a picture of the Bond actors on the next page, so we visited Google images and he decided on a picture of the complete set of DVD covers for the Bond films. I printed it off and he cut it to fit the page. Then I asked him to write the names of the actors around the edges and draw arrows to the appropriate actors' faces.

By this time, he had had enough of the project, so I didn't push it any further. But he did say, 'I can take this to school and show my teachers.'

And that's all I wanted – for him to be proud of something he'd produced from his own creative drive.

Tip

Think of a project which would stir your child to action and create an end-product they could be proud of. With Jamie it's films. But with your child it might be dinosaurs, airplanes, steam engines, colours or animals. The important thing is to try to incorporate your child in the project – have a picture of your child 'thinking' or 'saying' things about the subject in speech bubbles. If you have an IT friend, ask them to help the child create his/her own webpage.

CHAPTER 25

Encouraging Conversation with Games and Puzzles

We all know the enjoyment we get from games – board games, sport, card games and so on – but do we actually realise the importance of games? They teach team spirit, allow you to share quality time, show your child respect in action, teach turn-taking, and most importantly for our children, offer opportunities for communication. In fact, if ever you're at a loss of what to do with your child, look around for a game to play.

There are many opportunities for enrolling your child in sporting activities and it's a good idea to take advantage of as many as you can. There is an organisation called Special Olympics which operates world-wide, and through them we found several sports to take Jamie to, but I only enrolled him in two or, at most, three a week at any one time. My rationale was that overkill could stress him and I would be strung out trying to get him to all these meetings during the week. In fact, whenever I weighed up the things I wanted to do with Jamie, minimum effort won out. I never created a situation where he was likely to get tense.

So, I enrolled him in judo and soccer when he was six. He dropped out of judo within a few months. He just couldn't understand the rules and was completely unable to sit for the oral test. However, he continued with soccer for several years, starting with a regular club but then moving to the Special Olympics team. He had some trouble at soccer, doing well at training where they played in pairs and organised groups, but the real games every Saturday were torture for him and for me. He often fled the pitch in tears because the guys weren't passing to him. I tried to explain to him that you had to call out and put yourself in a 'good' position, but it was too much. The solution: Jamie only went to training sessions from then on.

Apart from fitness activities, we also played card and board games. These are just as valuable yet seem to have been replaced by computer and online games. Now I'm not against computer games, but there are certain aspects of 'real-time' play which cannot be replicated.

We are a family of game players. When Jamie was very young, I got him playing Uno, Rummy and Snakes and Ladders, all the time reinforcing the play with comments and encouragers: 'It's your turn.' 'You need a red five.' 'Oh, down you go!' 'What number is that?' There are so many opportunities for communication that it's impossible to list them all – numbers, counting, colours, comparative adjectives (better, worse), ordinals (first, second, etc.) as well as the 'nobler' principles of ethics, fairness, honesty and trust.

A few years later, our family began playing Eurogames. These are a collection of quite complicated games that involve cards, dice, boards, fantasy scenarios and so on. Jamie didn't join in these games and would usually be left to do a jigsaw on his own. However, I went searching the web for other Eurogames and came up with some stunningly simple ones, which, when we actually played them, were perfect for Jamie to ace at. There was one particular game called 'Ricochet Robots', where you had to move a little robot around the board ricocheting off the edges and 'walls' put up in his way to reach a nominated 'goal' square. It was so enjoyable to have Jamie involved and actually winning.

I also discovered a specialist games store and whenever Jamie had money for his birthday or I felt like treating him due to his points score during the week, we'd head off for the store and look through the offerings. That store carried a lot of what I call 'physical Tetris' games – where you had to recreate a puzzle picture by shifting coloured plastic pieces around or you had to play against someone else and win at 3D noughts and crosses. The games were on display and could be played with beforehand, and Jamie found this place endlessly fascinating.

And don't forget word games like Boggle and Scrabble. Although Jamie was poor at comprehension, he revelled in anagrams. Perhaps now he's ready for crosswords...

Tips

Don't sign your child up for too much per term.

Let go if your child isn't enjoying the sport.

Buy a book of simple, regular card games and try them.

Don't assume your child can't cope with a game your older family enjoys. Invite your child to play and you may be surprised.

Ask the teacher about games they've got in the classroom – often they're particularly suited to that age group and capability.

Subscribe to specialist toy/game producers' catalogues which will provide you with ideas for gifts and activities.

Take your child to a specialist toy/game shop and let them choose a game regularly as a treat for earning points.

PART II

Developing Social Skills, Life Skills and Independence

CHAPTER 26

Making Friends

Making friends was always going to be difficult for Jamie and the problems haven't lessened as he's got older. He always knew he wanted friends but didn't know the basics of what one *did* with friends. He couldn't understand concepts of loyalty, secret sharing, giggling, jokes, trust – even outings with friends. It simply wasn't enough to place him with peers and let him be naturally drawn to someone.

I decided that the best places to start were sporting clubs. So when he was six, I enrolled him in judo and soccer at local clubs. It didn't go well. He felt affronted when he had to 'fight' other boys at judo, then got very angry when he lost. He couldn't understand the practice pushing and pulling games with ropes and was never going to pass the initial test which involved a simple oral exam on the principles of judo ('be fair', 'do your best', etc.). Now that I look back on that period, I wish I had already started conversation work with him. We could have rehearsed or scripted the exchanges that were necessary in the oral exams. However, it was years later that I thought of helping him address his problems directly.

Around the same time, Jamie joined a soccer club. He was reasonable at the training sessions because he could see what the other boys were doing and copy them, and there was a lot of pair work which he did quite well. But the actual games were another matter. He didn't have a clue that he had to run and get the ball. He waited on the sidelines, hoping the boys would kick it to him. Again and again I told him, 'You have to shout and ask for the ball. You have to put yourself in a good position and they will pass it to you.' But, with typical self-effacement, Jamie just stood there throughout the game, getting more and more confused and upset because it wasn't like training. He did continue at soccer for a few more seasons, but he quickly dropped out of the Saturday games and just continued with weekday training.

I also thought of other clubs, but I realised quite quickly that I couldn't enrol Jamie in regular activities like scouts or boys' brigade. However, when I heard about Special Olympics, I enrolled him in our local branch. This organisation provides sporting activities for children and adults with Special Needs. They offered golf, tennis, swimming, basketball, horseriding and soccer. I enrolled Jamie in golf, which was held at a driving range. Jamie found this very dull and we stopped going after a year. He had more success with tennis and continued for several years, dropping out only when he left school.

These activities brought him 'hobbies' or 'weekly dates' but not really friends. He didn't get close to anyone on the teams. He never had sleepovers and rarely got invited to birthday parties. Whenever Jamie had a party, I'd invite the players from Special Olympics but he never expressed a desire to see them on his own.

There was one activity that he did enjoy – Big Night Out. This was a monthly disco held in a scout hall, organised by a music therapist at the special school. With loud music, a raging DJ, pizza and ice-cream and a crowded dance floor, Jamie was delirious. He discovered himself through music.

As far as Jamie's social life is concerned, I wish I'd had my time over. I would have followed Nuala Gardner's approach as outlined in her memoir, *A Friend Like Henry*. She had a child who was far more severely autistic than Jamie, yet she took him again and again to group activities for children. She even moved house so that he could be on an estate where he was likely to form friendships (and he did). She refused to accept the embarrassment she often felt for her son and continued to expand his world. I wish I'd done that and enrolled Jamie in a wider range of classes and ones that demanded his socialising or verbalising – like choir, drama classes, theatre productions, music lessons.

The thing is – once the time of childhood is past, a time where you can impose your will on your child and drive them to events and insist that they take part or at least try something new, that time never returns. Jamie is left with Facebook 'friends' and workmates.

Tips

Get your son or daughter involved in as many activities as possible as early as possible.

Try not to despair of the many failures you're setting your child up for.

Be there with them and debrief the situation afterwards.

Find out the names and phone numbers of the children at the events and get in touch with them.

CHAPTER 27
Dealing with Authority Figures

It has always been difficult for Jamie to obey authority figures. When he was little, the psychologists called him 'oppositional'. As he grew older, he would just take offence at something a teacher or carer said as he misunderstood so much of what he heard. Additionally, he reacted badly to loud voices.

This sensitivity to sound is apparently common in children with Asperger's but it made Jamie's classroom time very difficult with teachers shouting to ensure noisy students could hear them. It's also difficult to explain politely to teachers that a loud voice only makes Jamie's understanding worse.

The main problem was getting Jamie to accept the 'No' word. He reacted badly every time when he was young, getting more and more frustrated. This happened often at home but even more frequently at school. He just couldn't stand it.

I ended up taking Jamie to a clinic for children with Oppositional Defiant Disorder. I don't know whether that's what he had but the process was for us both to go into a sectioned-off part of a room where there were toys and playthings. The 'section' had walls and a door. He and I were to play in this room until I told him not to do something and he said 'No'. As soon as he said 'No', I was to go out of the room. Jamie regularly had a meltdown when I disappeared. He cried and cried as he couldn't see me or hear me.

It was meant to teach him that his 'No' had consequences and he couldn't just refuse to do things (or not do things) I wanted. But he was so young – just four years old – and language meant nothing to him. It didn't seem to improve his behaviour and I've often wondered whether it left him with a sense of insecurity.

So when he enrolled in school, his disposition was hardly better and he resented being told what to do by teachers even more than he did by me. He was often scolded at school and asked to sit in the corner or denied treats such as outings, but his resentment of authority figures became absolute when he came across a deputy principal in his early teens.

This woman only taught the class once or twice a week, but spoke loudly and roughly. She found it highly amusing to insult the pupils in a mock-friendly way, little realising that the students had no understanding of sarcasm or irony. For Halloween, Jamie worked on creating a mask to wear to school. As he walked through the gates, she took it off him and told him he was rude and frightening. She could have said kindly, 'That mask is very well done but it might frighten the younger students. Take it off and I'll keep it for you for after school.' Her abrupt manner upset him and he cried about it to me that night.

After several months of this kind of treatment, Jamie grew to dread Thursdays when she taught his class. He never understood her jokes and didn't know how to respond to her. He was always coming to me and complaining about her. Worse than that, he started swearing at her and then I was called in from work to collect him for time out from school.

Finally, I sat him down and explained to him my understanding of the situation: 'You don't like Mrs X. She talks rudely to you and your friends. But you won't always have her as your teacher. In the future you won't see her again and she'll never be able to tell you off again.' His eyes brightened. 'Also,' I continued, 'you have a good heart' – putting my hand on his chest – 'but you mustn't have a bad mouth' – putting my fingers on his lips. He seemed then to understand the fact that it was not acceptable to swear and the incidents of bad language decreased.

I also took him through intonation patterns or exercises to help him learn to express his anger at this teacher in an acceptable way to authority figures. When he told me what he said to them, I repeated it in a gentler intonation and added the person's name to it, for example: 'I didn't do it!' became 'I didn't do it, Mrs X.'

Of course the teachers often got angry with him because he was ranting against other kids in the playground, thinking they were bullying him. For this, I got him to create his own swear words – words that no-one else would know were swear words. He came up with: 'Bite my blood-boned body!!', which I thought was pretty good. We also shared other 'bad sayings', such as: 'Jobber-knobber-piper's-son!' and 'Rassen-tassen-frassen!' I realised that if I could get him to substitute weird sayings for really bad swear words, he wouldn't get into trouble as often.

Tips

Encourage your child to invent their own 'swear' words that won't upset the teacher.

Repeat your child's angry rants in a modulated tone so that they understand the way that language can reflect its purpose.

Explain that this situation won't last forever and the particular teacher who's worrying your child will not be there for good.

Think of your own relationship with your child's teachers and make sure that your dealings with the teachers are always exemplary, particularly when your child is around.

CHAPTER 28

Birthday Parties and Youth Groups

Birthday parties are ideal events for socialising: playing games, having competitions, opening presents, expressing thanks and so on. Each year I would try to organise a different kind of party for Jamie. Sometimes it was a trip to a theme park with a school friend, while other times it was a McDonald's birthday gathering led by an enthusiastic McDonald's employee who kept the troops happy.

The best party I ever organised though, was undoubtedly the fancy dress/Halloween party I arranged when Jamie was 11. Normally, I wouldn't recommend fancy dress parties – they take a lot of organising for busy parents. But I got in touch with each parent beforehand and asked whether it would be too much trouble to get or make an outfit and I limited the numbers to five.

As Jamie's birthday falls on 1 November, I was able to hold a trick-or-treat evening with me accompanying the kids on their tour around the neighbourhood. And I did a letter-drop in the street a few days before, advising neighbours that Jamie and his friends would be calling on them. Virtually all the locals had read the message and got stocks of treats in for the boys. A couple of them even had a separately wrapped present for the birthday boy.

As it was Halloween, I went online and looked for recipes that were suitable – spiders' biscuits, witches' fingers, gooey green jelly and so on. And I researched games that could be played at any time – wrap the mummy, bob apple, pass the parcel and bouncing on the trampoline. Naturally, I decked the house out with ghoulish masks, spiders' webs and Dracula capes and got Jamie to help.

Of course your child's birthday may not coincide with a particular festival but you can organise an 'un-birthday' celebration where several friends are invited to your son or daughter's party.

Naturally, I helped Jamie prepare for the day by talking to him about what was going to happen and by getting him involved in the preparations. So we talked beforehand about the future: 'Who is coming?' 'What colour balloons do you want?' 'What kind of food shall we prepare?' 'What did you do at Nathan's birthday party?' Then during the party I let him take a lot of photos and afterwards we spent a pleasant hour discussing what had happened: 'What was Stuart wearing?' 'How many pieces of cake did you eat?' 'Who got a wet face from the bob apple game?'

About a week later I got the photos printed and together Jamie and I put them in a special album. We relived the party through our conversation and added more ideas for what we would do next time: 'Who would you invite next time?' 'Which games would you play?' We even drew up a mind-map with ideas on this particular party and for future parties.

As Jamie grew older, I realised how sociable he really was and how much he enjoyed company. Yet he could not make friends himself, so I rang a local church I'd heard about which had a Youth Group and enrolled Jamie there. I spoke to the organiser of Madshack (the name of the group) on the phone and explained Jamie's condition, and Jamie went to their first meeting. He was about 14 and had never attended anything without me, yet it was clear that mothers were not invited.

We drove up and there were 70–80 kids in and around the hall. They were on their phones, skateboarding or chatting in the darkness. The whole hubbub disconcerted me because I knew Jamie couldn't stand noise. Anyway, we found our way to Josh, the organiser, who was surrounded by kids and

I cheerily said good-bye to Jamie. I was so anxious about leaving him there alone, but I told myself again and again that he would be fine, that he needed to practise meeting new people on his own and that I had given him enough preparation to socialise. I sat at home wondering what they were doing and how he was getting on. Then I went back and arrived half an hour before the meeting ended.

I found Jamie in a prayer room with half a dozen other guys. They'd been talking about 'men's matters'. Josh was enthusiastic. They'd had a movie quiz and Jamie had brought in all the answers for his team. He was welcomed and applauded as a great team member. My happiness was overflowing. Jamie had found his place here.

Madshack continued for another three years and every so often we'd meet strangers in the supermarket or mall and Jamie would greet them, then tell me he'd met them at Madshack. I was worried about Madshack ending – teenagers couldn't go to the meetings after the age of 18 – but it ended by Jamie's own initiative: he found that he couldn't believe in a Christian God so he didn't want to be a hypocrite and asked not to go any more.

I would like to say that Madshack and the parties were followed up by sleepovers and get-togethers with these friends, but Jamie remained painfully shy and never wanted to instigate a meeting with a friend himself. He continued to agree to arrangements I had made with his friends from school but steadfastly refused to organise anything himself. Now that he's 18 and in a situation where it's less acceptable for mothers to arrange outings or meetings, his social life remains circumscribed and it's an issue we're still working on.

Tips

Make your child's birthday parties as different as possible from each other – but don't knock yourself out trying to organise huge celebrations every year.

Make the most of the conversational opportunities parties offer for your child.

Find out where the nearest youth groups are and, when you think your child is mature enough to cope, let them join one.

CHAPTER 29

Planning for Practical Life Skills

Throughout this book, I have suggested how important it is to prepare things in advance – either for the next day or for the following week. This becomes even more important when forward planning over long periods of time.

As in every good campaign, it's good to know what your goals are. So when Jamie was about 14, I wrote down the practical things I'd like him to be able to do by the time he was 21:

1. Look after himself in the home/prepare for each day.

2. Do his own washing/drying/ironing of clothes.

3. Do his own shopping.

4. Do his own cooking.

5. Be able to take public transport.

6. Be able to drive a car.

7. Leave home and live an independent life.

This last goal may seem harsh or unreachable, but I know in the bottom of my heart that I want Jamie to be able to live without me. It's the nightmare of all parents of children with disabilities – how will they survive when we're gone?

So I kept these goals in mind and began to work towards them. Some things arose gradually – the shopping and the cooking, for example. Others took a long, long time to work on – like driving a car.

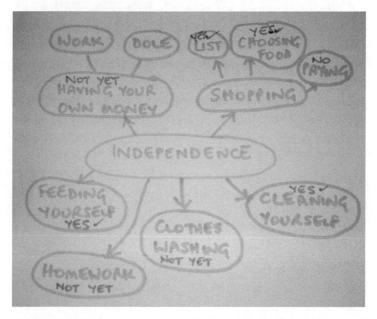

Using public transport also took some time, but it's a good example of how I planned around Jamie's skill base. At the time I was eligible for respite care, so once a week I could have a carer for two or three hours. The not-for-profit organisation was very respectful and was keen to organise a person Jamie felt happy with to train Jamie in any way I wanted.

I decided I wanted Jamie to learn how to catch a bus to and from his school. It was July and I set a goal for Jamie to be able to catch buses on his own by the following January. (I didn't tell Jamie or put any pressure on him.) Normally I would take Jamie in the car to school. It was a run I'd done for the whole of his school life so it was quite alien for him to do anything else. I first fanned the flames of independence in Jamie himself – we used to drive past the other students waiting at the bus stop and Jamie would wave and call out to them.

'Wouldn't it be nice,' I'd say, 'if you could catch the bus with them?'

'Er…no… It's a long way.' Or he'd say it was hot. Or he'd say it was slow or crowded. He definitely did not want to do it. Nevertheless, I took Jamie on a few trips into and out of the city by bus and then we interviewed a carer and I booked him for every Monday afternoon. Jamie's route home meant that he had to catch two buses – the carer would turn up at Jamie's school, choose the right bus and show Jamie how to pay the fares.

One carer was too determined to teach Jamie the ropes and kept repeating the same questions to him: 'Which bus number do you catch to the city? Where do you get off? Where do you walk to? Which bus number do you catch home?' And so on.

After a few weeks of this, Jamie was furious. 'He always tells me! I know!'

So I simply said, 'Do you want to do it on your own now?'

'Yes!'

I was stunned and rather worried. I rang the school and explained that now, in November, Jamie wanted to catch the bus on his own. He was 16. He should be able to manage. However, I asked the teachers to watch out for him. I also made sure he knew how to ring me on his mobile.

I was so grateful when Jamie did come home safely on that first trip. I couldn't believe it had all gone well. It was an anxious time for me and it wasn't all plain sailing. There were times when he caught the wrong bus or caught the right bus heading in the wrong direction.

As the hands of the clock sped round to 4 o'clock, I'd become anxious and at 4pm I'd ring him.

'Hmm… Mum, I'm at the 7-Eleven.'

'Right. I'll collect you.' And I'd head off to fetch him. At least he had a good sense of direction and was familiar with the roads around the inner-city suburbs. It made it a lot easier to find him, but there must have been at least six occasions when he got lost.

However, by the time six months had passed and January came around, Jamie was well familiar with the routes, times and fares of all buses to the city. He began to take the bus into the city at the weekends to go shopping by himself and the convenience for me of not having to take him to school every day was liberating.

Tips

Make a rough list of all the things you would like your child to be able to do.

Make a plan of when you hope to be able to have them achieve those goals.

Share your plans and ideas with family, friends and acquaintances. (It was friends of mine who told me about the respite care facility.)

Make sure your child knows how to use a mobile phone before carrying out any plans that involve separation.

CHAPTER 30

Using Mind-Maps to Develop Abstract Life Skills

One night after I'd had a chat with Jamie about resilience and independence, I went to bed thinking about the qualities we had talked about. I was drifting off when I suddenly thought of mind-maps. I had used mind-maps earlier to help him with his vocabulary and conversation. Now perhaps I could use it to help him learn about maturity.

As I explained in Chapter 19, mind-maps are idea generators which are a valuable tool in thought showering and are easy to create. Using a blank piece of paper, you write the subject of your thoughts in the middle of the page in a circle. You then think of all related ideas and draw arrows and circles to new ideas. The best way to generate ideas is to think of the answers to the Who? What? When? Where? Why? and How? questions (e.g. Who will do it? Who is affected? Who was there? etc.).

So the next day I bought a huge scrapbook and four brightly coloured pens. I sat down with Jamie and opened a page. 'Now,' I said, 'do you remember last night when you earned extra points?'

He nodded.

'Well, we're going to write down our ideas about growing up and becoming a man. What do you think a mature person does?'

'He listens to his mum?'

'Hmmm… Well, that's interesting. Because when you listen to your mum and do what your mum says, that's being a good *child*. But when you're an adult, you make decisions for yourself. You decide what you do and you don't have to be obedient to anyone.'

Jamie smiled at this.

'What we're going to do is talk about Life Skills. Do you know what Life Skills are?'

'No.'

'They are the skills that let you live your own life and be happy. There are four main skills: Resilience, Independence, Maturity and Sociability.' I wrote down the words 'Life Skills' in the centre of the page and four arrows from it to the circled words Resilience, Independence, Maturity and Sociability. I started with maturity since Jamie had known that word for years after reading video cases which stated 'For mature audiences only'.

'What is maturity?'

'You are kind.'

'Yes. Very good.' And I wrote that down in another circle. 'Being generous is also a sign of maturity. That means helping others and giving your time or money to them.' I added 'generous'.

'What else?' I asked. 'What else does a mature person do?'

'Helps his mum,' said Jamie.

'That's right. We'll write "helpful."' And I wrote it in a circle off 'Maturity'. 'And what else does a mature person do?'

'Says "Please" and "Thank you".'

'Yes, a mature person is polite, so we'll write that down here. A grown-up knows when to say "please" and "thank you". He doesn't have to have his mummy telling him.'

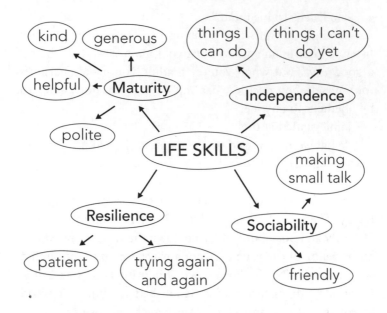

The mind-map was growing. 'Now let me tell you about Independence. Do you know what Independence is?'

'No.'

'It means you can do things on your own. Now let's think – what things can you do on your own?'

No reply.

'Can you shower yourself?'

'Yes.'

'Good. We'll write that down under "things I can do"... Can you drive a car?'

'No, don't be silly.'

'No, you can't. But when you're a man, you'll be able to drive a car. So we'll put "driving a car" under the things you can't do – at the moment.'

And so we continued until we had built up the mind-map with me asking and Jamie answering simple questions. I explained the major difficult concepts but made sure I gave examples from his own daily life or asked him for examples.

At the end, I said, 'Now we have a picture of what a mature person is like and what they can do. And look, if we just tick off what you can do, you'll see you're becoming more and more mature.' And so saying, I ticked off 'polite', 'shower myself', and so on. Jamie was so proud of it, we pinned it to the back of his bedroom door and as the months went by, we added more abilities and ticked them off.

Tip

When you have a child who can read and write and you want to explain or reinforce something, think of mind-maps. Almost every idea can be explored through mind-mapping and it allows the child to add their own observations or contribute to the exercise. It also means it is likely to remain in their memory for much longer.

I used mind-mapping with Independence, Resilience, Maturity and Sociability here. These sound very abstract to a person with speech and language problems, but you can explain these concepts and explore them in very simple terms.

CHAPTER 31

Organising Daily Life and Establishing a Routine

Nowadays schools are so demanding, you're quite likely to get a request for the ingredients to a four-course meal for the following day. It usually happens when the shops are closed and your fridge and pantry are empty.

It's an exaggeration, but it does seem to me more and more that bringing up a family is like running a small business. There are forms to sign, fêtes to attend, cakes to bake, permission slips to return, uniforms to buy, waivers to agree to, interviews to have, homework to check, sports days to attend, emails to answer, stationery to stock up on, and so on and so on. As the weight of this correspondence and activity is carried by the parents, it's unthinkable to believe that one day your own child will be able to do all this when they become a parent or even when they leave home and runs their own life. The demands may be different but the responsibilities and processes are similar.

Many children with Asperger's like routines and some even crave them. The difficulty for a parent is to shoulder all that responsibility but not forget that the child should be encouraged to assume whatever responsibilities they can. This is what will make all the difference in your child becoming truly independent.

As I indicated before, a calendar is always useful. Keep it in your child's bedroom to write down things for them to look forward to in the coming weeks. As soon as they are able, get them to write down forthcoming events. If a birthday is coming up, write that in (e.g. 'Cath's B-day') and then get your child to work out when they should buy the card and gift (say, ten days before write on 'Cath's present'). If your child's handwriting is too big or the calendar is too small, use the calendar on the computer or paint a kitchen wall with blackboard paint and chalk out the days of the month. This activity will consolidate your child's knowledge of the passing days, too.

When Jamie was younger, he often woke up very early in the morning. He'd get up and pace around the room, muttering indistinctly and suddenly bursting out with laughter. It was weird and rather disturbing to listen to. I wanted to stop this practice and I talked to a friend of mine. She asked me to look at possible causes of his early morning wake-ups. Could it be the curtains were too thin and letting in the sunlight? Was he being disturbed by the dog? Did he want to go to the toilet? I tried to establish if any of these were the cause, but it looked like, no, he was simply getting up early now.

Then she suggested I create an early morning quiet box of activities that he could do to help him pass the time before waking up the rest of the household. So I got together a collection of things he liked playing with:

- a couple of puzzles

- a couple of special books (only to be read at this time)

- paper, pens, colouring books

- a 'diary' for him to write in (he rarely did)

- battleships game.

I found that this meant he could play happily until the rest of the household woke up and he stopped 'talking' to himself once he was busy with these activities.

For breakfast, lunch and dinner, I quickly got Jamie into a routine of what to eat. Breakfast and lunch menus were usually the same: Weetabix and toast for breakfast; cheese or ham roll for lunch. Dinner varied according to what I'd planned. But Jamie's lunches for school were prepared by him the night before. I'd buy a selection of sandwich meats or spreads, mini-cheeses, an apple or orange, a cooling fruit juice, nuts and raisins and, as soon as Jamie was able, I'd get him to collect together and prepare the foodstuffs for his lunch the next day. In this way, Jamie got used to taking responsibility for his lunch and only rarely did he forget to make it.

As Jamie got older, his days at school became more organised. A school timetable showed what he did each day and he had to go prepared for certain subjects. I mean sports days where he had to take his sports uniform, catering/home economics where he had to take ingredients and on special Free Dress Days (non-uniform days) where he had to take a donation to charity. To help him prepare, I wrote on his calendar and reminded him the night before to pack whatever he needed. After a while, he consulted the calendar and got used to thinking about his catering/sporting needs with a simple prompt like: 'So what day is it tomorrow?'

The same went for homework. I kept in touch with teachers regularly by email and always knew what homework was due and when. As Jamie got into the higher grades and was responsible for larger-scale projects, I broke the project down into its component parts and wrote up a list of 'To do' jobs on it. Then he went down the checklist (usually with me helping him) and ticked off as each part was completed.

As Jamie got to 16, I thought it would be useful for him to learn to touch type so I set him a five-minute task each night to work on his touch typing. I can't say he thanked me and he never got past 22 words per minute, but I thought it was one more skill to add to his growing list for the future. Similarly, when he reached the right age, he started working on the online theory test for his driving licence.

All these nightly habits became a routine and because they were regular – every school night – and short, Jamie rarely acted up and complained. In his later years at high school, I made sure that he didn't do any evening extra-curricular activities, such as golf or judo, so that he could finish his regular tasks.

Try to alert your child as much as possible about what's going to happen at various events, but don't be over-organised and find yourself constantly nagging.

One of the best tips I ever got on my own self-management was to visualise what's going to happen, who will be there, what the seating arrangements will be and so on – to do a mental 'walk-through' of the event.

You can do the same with your child at night after bedtime reading: 'So, it's Uncle Bob's birthday on Saturday. Where are we going?'

'Grandma's.'

'What have we got for him?'

'A book.'

'Yes, and what will you say when you see him?... What will you wear?... What will you say when someone offers you some cake?' And so on. Later on you will be able to have more open-ended conversations starting with: 'Tell me what's going to happen at Uncle Bob's birthday.'

Basically, life runs more smoothly when it's predictable, but life is less interesting when it does that. And every time something goes wrong with the plans, it is bound to throw up more thoughts, challenges and opportunities that you can work on later. When Jamie was using a machine in woodwork one day, the teacher was alarmed because Jamie was obviously angry. The teacher took Jamie off the machine and rang me. Later that night, I explained to Jamie the dangers of operating machinery when you're upset and told him that must never happen again. 'But,' cried Jamie, 'that wasn't in the video!' The class had watched a training video on the 'do's' and 'don't's' of working with the machine and Jamie felt justifiably indignant because he hadn't been warned about this. The truth is, however much you plan and try to avoid problems, you can't risk-manage life.

Tips

Start by ensuring that things are prepared for the next day's activities and that your child is clear about what will happen. Slowly, after a few months (maybe years) of you organising your child and telling them what's going to happen, change it to questions you ask of them (e.g. 'What do you do on a Tuesday?' 'Where do you have to hand this form in?' 'What do you need?')

Ultimately, your goal is to ask your child the open-ended questions: 'So what's happening tomorrow?' and 'Are you ready?'

Use a calendar which he can write on.

Help your child visualise forthcoming events by asking them sensory questions, such as: 'What will that feel like?' 'What will he say?' and 'What will you see?'

Get into a routine with food times, homework, extra-curricular activities and projects.

Never expect your child to do tasks over an extended period of time.

Plan these activities for the same time of day – say, after snack time post-school.

Try not to feel down or disheartened when crises arise even at the most pre-planned events. A crisis will create other avenues to explore and other skills to consolidate. And disappointments for your child have to be expected and, in fact, should be welcomed in a way as opportunities for growth.

CHAPTER 32

Giving Your Child Responsibility for Daily Tasks

Many years ago, my mother was talking to me about the chaos in her friend's household every morning when her three children, but particularly her son Michael was racing around, to get out of the door for school. He regularly couldn't find his socks, needed his lunch in a hurry or had to get a form signed – all before they left the house, which should have been ten minutes ago. It made me think about breakfast chaos and how often we see it portrayed in movies.

Since then I have heard many mothers complaining about the 'busyness' of breakfast and how hassled they feel when pressured to feed, dress, prepare lunches and get kids off to school. However, I did work out a system of coping with weekday mornings in our household.

Jamie must have been about seven or eight. Each night before bed, I'd put out his clothes for him, check that they were washed and ironed, that he had a full set, that his sports uniform was out if necessary and check in his bag to see if there were any notes.

After a while of doing this, I thought, 'Why am I doing this? I can ask Jamie to get his clothes ready himself.' So I began helping him. I was still bathing him at this stage as he couldn't be relied on to wash himself properly. So as he undressed in the bathroom, I would take off each piece of clothing and ask him whether it was clean or dirty.

'Your shirt – is that clean?'

'Yes.'

'Did you wear it yesterday?'

'Yes.'

'Then it's not clean. Two days and it goes in the wash.'

'Two days.'

Then I told him that underpants and socks *always* went in the wash and so on. It has taken him many years to get the hang of washing and when it needs to be done, but he learnt very quickly that dirty clothes get put in the laundry basket so we have avoided the teenage complaints of 'Where are my jeans?' when everything's in a pile on the floor in front of them. In fact, because I started early with Jamie, I never faced the problems I've had with my teenage girls of wading through a pile of unwashed laundry on their bedroom floor. As Becca has said to me many times, 'I wish you'd trained me half as well!'

Once we'd got dirty clothing out of the way, I started on what Jamie was to wear the next day. At first it was painfully slow, but as with all things it takes more time at the beginning and saves you a lot of time later.

So, I'd open the wardrobe and say, 'What will you need for tomorrow?' (I didn't say this at weekends – I don't believe in giving kids too many choices too early. At weekends, I'd say, 'Now get out your blue T-shirt and grey shorts,' for the following day.) So on school nights, he started to take out his shirt, shorts, socks and shoes and underpants one by one and we both laid them on the bed together or hung them on the wardrobe door. This meant that by the time Jamie was eight, he was putting out his clothes for the next day and getting dressed without help in the morning.

As I have said before, I attacked the problem of school lunches by preparing them beforehand with Jamie (see p.116). At his new school they insisted on a 'cool box', which turned out to be a good investment. Not only is it sturdier than a regular lunch box, it also keeps the food fresh in the summer heat and you can put an ice-block in it. It comes with a useful handle for carrying as well.

Pretty soon after this, Jamie was making his own sandwiches and I only had to remind him to do it before he went to bed the night before. After a while, he asked if he could make them in the morning and he happily does this and has only forgotten his lunch once or twice.

With dressing and preparing lunch out of the way, there is no reason for Jamie to be late for school and he has the additional benefit of spending his time before school doing what he wants to.

Tip

Get your child into clear routines early on. It's often easier for our children to develop good habits because they like routines. Start slowly with manageable tasks like sorting the dirty clothes from clean ones, then build up to putting their clothes out for the next day, and preparing their own lunches. If you do it the night before, the anxiety and stress is taken out of breakfast time.

CHAPTER 33

Preparing Your Child to Organise Their Life

There comes a point when you realise your child really should be becoming an independent operator in life. With most children without autism this happens gradually as bit by bit you let them take over their own life (or alternatively, they take control themselves). But as parents of children with autism we automatically put off this day and continue to operate as if our child were incapable. He or she is not incapable – they just need more training to do tasks and we need to make a particular effort to notice when the time is right to prepare them for liaising with the outside world.

Just think of all that you have become accustomed to doing for them – buying their food, making their appointments, opening their correspondence, ferrying them to their various commitments, such as sport, music or church, filing, photocopying, phoning and so on. This organisation can be overwhelming even to an adult but, if it is introduced item by item, your child will feel the pride of achievement and responsibility.

On one occasion I came home from an overseas trip. There was a pile of mail for me and a few items for Jamie. There was a flyer from a charity, a bank statement and a newsletter from his athletics group. Instead of opening them for him, I handed them one by one to him.

'What do you want me to do with this?' he asked.

'Open it and read it.'

It was the flyer.

'What's it say?'

'What does this line say?' I asked in return.

'Please give generously to...'

'So what do you think they want?'

'They want money?' he asked uncertainly.

'Yes, they do. It's from a charity. They would like you to give some of your money to them. Would you like to do that?'

'Er... No.'

'Okay. You can put that in the rubbish. Now the next one.'

He opened it and read it carefully. After a while he said, 'It's from my bank.' He knew he had a bank account because his maths teacher had suggested we open one for him to see what interest meant and we'd made a special trip a few weeks before. 'But what does it mean?'

'Well, look at these numbers. They're withdrawals. That means you've taken this money out of your account. Do you remember doing that?'

'Yes.'

'And this?'

'Yes.'

'Then this is the money that's gone into your account in this column – here and here and here. Is that right?'

'Er... Yes.'

'Well, if you agree with that, then you can see how much you've got left. That's here at the bottom.'

'So that's my money?'

'Yes.'

'Right.'

'So if you agree with the bank statement, then you file it...and it goes here in the filing cabinet under "J" for Jamie.'

'Oh.'

'Right... Now the next one is from your athletics group. Open it up.'

'It's just pictures.'

'Yes. It tells you what's going on in the group.' And I then went through some of the relevant stories he might be interested in.

Later I realised what a big step this was for Jamie. He was actually interacting with the world as it presented itself through correspondence. He didn't show much interest, but I invited him to do it more and more often so that he learnt how to read for some purpose.

A few days after this, we were in the car travelling to tennis. I suddenly realised that I needed to make a hair appointment for Jamie but the hairdresser was due to close in ten minutes. I thought of asking Jamie to make the appointment, but it seemed too difficult. Quickly, I ran through what he'd have to say (known), what the hairdresser would reply (predictable) and what she'd be likely to ask him (unknown). Knowing I couldn't overload him with information, I pared it down in my mind to what was the absolute minimum I could send him in with: Thursday, 4pm, trim, Jamie, no particular hairdresser... Could he remember that? Would he get confused and upset? I reckoned I could chance it.

'Okay, Jamie... We need to make an appointment with the hairdresser for you to have a trim.'

He just looked at me.

'You'll have to do it. You just say your name and say you want an appointment. Thursday at 4pm. Okay?'

He didn't move. He was decidedly uncomfortable but he will not disobey a direct order, so I said, 'Take my mobile out of my handbag... Now look up the hairdresser's number.'

He did it.

'Now ring and ask for Thursday at 4pm.'

'Can't you?'

'No, I'm driving.'

'When we get back?'

'No, the hairdresser's will be closed. And we need that appointment. If you can't understand anything, just pause and ask me.'

Reluctantly, he dialled the number. I heard all of his conversation. It was simple and clear and although he asked for Monday first and forgot the time, he was making sense. He muddled through it and I shone with pride. Jamie had made his first appointment. By himself.

Tip

Never let an opportunity pass you by when you can ask your son or daughter to do something for themselves that you had previously done for them. Think of them asking for their favourite DVD or Playstation game at the video shop – make them ring up themselves but give them adequate preparation.

CHAPTER 34

What Your Child Can Learn from Caring for a Pet

As anyone knows who has read Nuala Gardner's incomparable book, *A Friend Like Henry*, pets can make a tremendous difference to a young child's life. In her book, she talks about how her son, who has severe autism, came out of himself and started to relate to their pet labrador, Henry. It is a truly moving story.

My girls tried to persuade me to get a dog for a long time. We got a cat when Jamie was about four, but he never bonded with Panther and Panther was always Caitie's cat. (In fact Jamie once threw Panther in the empty swimming pool in winter – I think he just wanted to experiment and see what happened. Fortunately, Panther scrambled out.) So when, a few years later, Becca and Caitie started lobbying in earnest, I thought seriously about it.

Since I was working at home and could be there with a puppy, it was a possibility. However, I was worried about Jamie. He had always been nervous around animals, particularly dogs. He fretted and squealed and generally made dogs excited with his nerves. I knew he was frightened of them, but I thought perhaps that was even more reason to bring one into our family, so a month before Jamie's fifth birthday, Caitie and I went to the dog pound and found Odin, a dachshund/terrier cross with a fretful bark and a nervous disposition. (I learnt later that it's best to choose the calmest dog available as they are less likely to cause problems or get upset. However, the die was cast and Odin came home with us.)

I put him in Caitie's bedroom and she calmed him and petted him. Once I'd collected Jamie, I talked to him about the new dog and explained how we'd have to look after him, what meals he'd have, where he'd sleep, how excitable he was and so on. I impressed upon him that we had to keep him calm, but Jamie was totally alarmed when he went into the bedroom. He squealed and kind of jabbed Odin as if to see if he really existed. Of course, Odin got more and more excited and started barking. It was not a good beginning.

As the days went by, I got Jamie to be less anxious around Odin and encouraged him to stroke him and pet him gently. I let Caitie do the feeding and playing with balls and toys, but after a while we decided it would be a good idea to enrol Odin in RSPCA training. The whole family went, which was probably not a good idea as we over-awed the dog. However, he did learn to sit, drop and stay so I could show Jamie how obedient Odin was and how important it was that he obeyed commands. The words 'obedient' and 'obedience' became part of Jamie's vocabulary and it was a useful way to illustrate how instructions can be followed.

From the start I got the kids involved in caring for Odin. I bought the dog food and showed Jamie how to feed him. We also had to clean up the mess – though that was usually left up to me (fair enough). But then there were the other things like making sure we hadn't left any 'nibbles' around the house for a young puppy to get at – shoes, pens, paper, linen. We were constantly defending our belongings against the curiosity of an eager pup.

I always made sure Jamie realised that Odin couldn't be played with like a toy – that he had rights and we had responsibilities. I think that's the great benefit and joy of owning a pet – that you give and get back in return. Odin always presented Jamie with a range of opportunities to practise or learn new skills. Odin needed walks and baths, tickles and discipline. And through these activities, Jamie grew to enjoy the responsibility of caring for some soul younger than him. As the youngest child in the family, he thoroughly enjoyed being the 'organiser', the 'leader' and the 'teller off'!

Looking back, it seems quite a short time before Jamie became quite comfortable around Odin. He probably calmed down around the time that Odin did. Now they play together happily and Odin always greets Jamie with special pleasure on his return home.

Tips

Take a while to make your decision as to whether you want a pet or not. There are many limitations they place on you.

Explain to your child, as far as you can, that you have to be quiet around a new pet, that they have to learn to trust you.

Let your child pet the animal so that they are making an immediate and physical contact with the animal. Often words are unnecessary to forging that bond.

Let your child help with the training of your pet and, as soon as they are old enough, let them become involved with feeding and grooming the pet.

CHAPTER 35

Preparing Your Child for Cooking

An essential part of an independent life for your child is being able to cook. Yet cooking is not an easy thing to do as so many skills are needed in preparing food to eat:

- Maths – measurements, temperatures, counting.

- Fine-motor skills – using cutlery, utensils.

- Literacy – reading words or identifying information via symbols.

- Concepts – hot, cold, sharp, safely.

- Language – understanding what 'fry', 'knife', 'bowl', 'pour', 'rise' and so on, really mean.

- Patience – not rushing to cut things up and get everything done so you can eat.

- Time – what is 30 minutes?

So, as you can see from the above, what most of us take for granted is not really an easy task at all.

With Jamie, I started in the general way that most parents do – by baking cakes or cooking a meal at the weekends and getting him to help me. He would measure out something or mix the ingredients together – just little tasks which contributed to the end product.

When Jamie was about 14, he went to stay with my elder daughter, Becca, and she started him on peeling vegetables. They were having roast and Becca taught Jamie how to prepare the carrots, sweet potato and potatoes. He complained heartily and explained that it would take too long. However, she just continued and, though the meal was delayed by an hour or so, he did complete the task. Ever since, I've asked him to peel the vegetables for our meals and he accepts it as his job. However, I did make sure the peeler was sharp and that he cut away from himself. (Remember that dull knives are more dangerous than reasonably sharp knives and serrated knives are even more dangerous because of the type of wound they make if you cut yourself.)

Of course, it's often best to involve your child from the beginning of the cooking process – by contributing to the shopping list. I get Jamie to check the cupboard with me and ask him if we have certain items. Then he can write the word on the list or (for younger kids) draw a picture on their own chalkboard.

As for preparing meals, I started with breakfast by asking Jamie what we needed for his meal of Weetabix and toast. We got the ingredients out – milk, cereal, bread, butter, spread – and I asked him what utensils and crockery we needed. Then I supervised as he mixed his cereal, milk and honey and toasted his bread. Within a short period of time, Jamie was making his own breakfast.

Many other meals involved frying – fish, sausages, bacon and so on – and this was the most difficult as the foods would spit hot oil at him. I had to stand over him and ensure that he didn't stand too close, didn't turn the heat up too high, and cooked the flesh evenly.

Make some rules for the kitchen and have them on display in the kitchen – things like: no running in the kitchen, how to hold a knife when moving from where the knife is kept to where you are working, don't overfill items such as kettles, saucepans and so on with hot liquid, make sure saucepan handles are put towards the back of the hotplate so you don't knock the saucepan off the stove. You can gain some good information on the internet about safety for children in the house or how to make your house safer for children.

Make flash cards showing the item (cutlery, utensils, crockery, food items etc.) in picture form with the word underneath or above, depending on how your child best sees and comprehends the flash card. So perhaps you need to have a large picture and the word underneath or a medium-sized picture and the word quite large above. You can get the pictures from images on the web.

When I was considering concepts like measurement and safety, again I talked about things first. I put colour or shape codes on measuring jugs and spoons so that specific measurements were easily identified. For example, you could put a yellow dot at the 250ml and a blue dot on the 500ml marks and so on and this coding should also be on the recipe itself. If your child doesn't identify colours, use shapes instead or perhaps animal pictures (the sheep is 250ml, the cow is 500ml etc.).

I also suggest that the kitchen cupboards be organised logically – perhaps putting all the baking things together in one cupboard, keeping the measuring jug, scales and measuring spoons in one place and so on. If your child can find the items easily, it encourages them to participate and sets them up for success and not failure.

Think about how you are asking your child to do things – instructions should be kept short and simple to start with, and use your manners: 'Please get the measuring jug from the cupboard.' 'Thank you, could you now get the mixing bowl for me?' and so on. To help your child, you could even put pictures of what is in the cupboards on the cupboard doors.

Remember, just because you cut up your carrots with a knife, this might not be the ideal way for you child to do it – perhaps a food processor would be more suitable and safe for them? However, when starting to use knives, start with a knife that is not too big and has a handle which suits your child's hands. Stand next to them – with a knife too – and then show them step by step how to cut. Start by cutting things which are not really hard or round-shaped as they roll around and are more likely to cause an accident. Toast or a cake are great foods to practise cutting with a reasonably sharp knife. You need to cut on a flat, non-slip surface and you need to hold the item with your fingers out of the way. You can buy a stainless steel sandwich cutter to put over the sandwich – one which has a slot for the knife (industrial or commercial kitchen shops sell these). And when your child does graduate to slicing hard foods like carrots, you might like to cut them in half longways first so that there is a flat side to stop them moving around.

If you have disappointments – say, a cake hasn't risen – don't make a fuss about it, just laugh it off and suggest you put more icing on the top to make it taste lovely. Keep your child focused on enjoying the experience and not thinking of it as a success or failure.

Once Jamie had a basic knowledge of the kitchen and how to help me prepare a few dishes, I decided that he could do the whole thing himself with me giving instructions from afar (instead of standing over him as he did it and taking over when it got too much). As I guided him through the steps, I suddenly hit upon the idea of a Recipe Book. When he leaves to live on his own, he will need to consult a recipe book – what better idea than one he has compiled himself of tried-and-true recipes that his mother has taught him?

So as he cooked, I took pictures of him. At the end I took a picture of the final plated meal. I printed two pictures and grabbed a regular exercise book and wrote 'Recipe Book' in the subject line on the front. Then, once we had eaten the meal, we sat together and he wrote down the recipe.

'This is for when you leave home and have to cook for yourself,' I said.

'How old will I be?'

'Oh, about 21.' (I thought it was a good idea to introduce a time-line for him to think of. Jamie loves dates and deadlines.)

Here is the recipe:

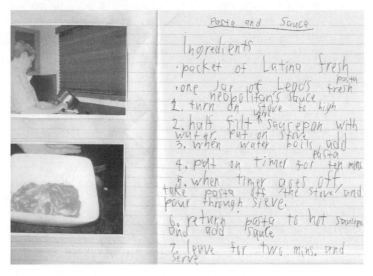

Pasta and Sauce

Ingredients
· packet of Latina fresh pasta fresh
· one jar of Lego's Neopolitan's Sauce
1. turn on stove to high
2. half filt Saucepan with water, put on stove
3. when water boils, add pasta
4. put on timer for ten mins.
5. when timer gets off, take pasta off the stove and pour through sieve.
6. return pasta to hot Saucepa and add Sauce
7. leave for two mins. and serve

It's a very, very basic recipe and I've included instructions that wouldn't be found in a regular cook book ('Turn on stove; put on timer for ten mins'). All these details give our future chefs guidance for absolutely every step so that they can't go wrong. Of course, the recipes have to be extremely simple but I hope Jamie's Recipe Book will be a real help to him in the years to come. Who knows? Maybe he'll become the expert shopper and chef that I've never been!

Tips

When considering how to teach your child to cook in a safe way there are some things you need to consider:

1. What are the child's fine-motor skills like – what implements are they currently using safely?

2. Do they understand concepts and consequences? Specifically, do they understand that if they put their hands on a hot surface, they will burn themselves or if they put a sharp knife on a part of their body, they will cut themselves?

3. Are you going to try to teach general cooking ideas? Or are you going to teach specific meals to cook? What is more important – trying to teach culinary arts in general or having your child create something quickly and simply, which they will see as a positive outcome?

4. What language does your child understand? Not only words such as 'hot', 'cold' and 'sharp', but measurements. What are their reading and comprehension skills like? If you gave them a recipe, would they not only be able to read it but also understand it? Do they read or do they need symbols or verbal prompts?

Then approach each of these skills in turn and help your child master them.

Ensure that you allow yourself time – do not try to do things when you are tired or have time limitations as this places pressure on you and you are more likely to lose patience and not consider the most important thing of all before you start – safety!

Although I think the Recipe Book is a great idea, don't overdo it. Jamie finds any writing a chore so I'll let him practise with recipes he's familiar with first and then every so often (say once or twice a month), we'll put an entry into the book.

After your child has practised with a certain menu a few times, when you come to write it down, make it a memory game of re-enacting what actually happened step by step.

Keep the Recipe Book in an accessible but separate place from the kitchen. You can put it with the Scrapbook and Project books.

CHAPTER 36

Preparing Your Child to Manage Money

A critic is a person who knows the price of everything and the value of nothing.

Oscar Wilde

There are two different concepts we want to teach our children about money: the cost of things and the value of things. The *cost* of items includes the maths of addition, subtraction, multiplication, division, percentages, rebates, discounts and so on. It involves cash and cash handling – transactions. The *value* of items involves our attitudes to money, finance, economics, saving, budgeting and so on. This determines whether our child is likely to save or be a spendthrift, generous or mean, a borrower or a lender.

Let's deal with the first concept – transactions. You may think these ideas are best left to the maths teacher, but in fact there is so much we can do to supplement what's taught in the classroom and we can do that through conversation. Conversation about cash will improve your child's understanding of mathematical concepts in general and will be helpful in the practical world of retail.

In retail both plastic and cash transactions are used. Children see real cash exchanges less and less often and this makes the trade more abstract and less easy for them to understand. In order to concretise transactions, make sure you use coins and notes when your child is with you. Then teach the coin/note breakdown of the amount you're paying. Later on you can move on to getting change and explain, outside the shop, the way to count 'up' to the given amount. For example, 'That cost $8.60 and I gave the shopkeeper $10 so we count up from $8.60, $8.70, $8.80, $8.90, $9.00 and another dollar makes the $10 I gave him.'

I also played money 'games' with Jamie. For example, Kim's game, where several items are shown on a tray for 30 seconds and then the tray is moved and one item is taken off it. Jamie had to guess what was missing – all the items were coins or notes.

We played guessing games when window shopping as to how much any item cost and what was a good buy or not. I suppose we played these games because I remembered the scene from the film *Rain Man* where Raymond, the autistic savant, guesses that a car cost a $100 and a Hershey bar cost the same. I'm pleased to say Jamie quickly caught on to different prices.

Later in Jamie's studies, when he was about 16, a private maths tutor was trying to teach him interest rates and said that he found it difficult to conceptualise gaining interest on savings, so she suggested opening a bank account for him. We did this – I put $200 in and every month, he'd open his bank statement and we'd see the additional 'earnings'. This had the added benefit of his entering the world of commerce for the first time – signing paperwork, getting a wallet to hold his cards (student card, ATM card, concession card, etc.). My son was growing up.

About the same time I broached the topic of discounts. We looked at the sale signs in shop windows – 30 per cent off, 10 per cent discount and so on. I asked Jamie general questions as we passed, like, 'Is 30 per cent off better than 20 per cent off?', 'Which shop has the best deals?' and so on. All this conversation followed on from his maths tutorials and fed into his understanding of costs and expenses.

I had taken the starter money for Jamie's bank account from an account that I'd opened for Jamie when he was three. Each week I'd been donating about $10 so that when he was 18 he had a pile of money to buy outright a second-hand car and pay for expenses like servicing, registration, insurance, roadside assistance and so on. This separate bank account is still going and will form the basis of a savings account from which Jamie can pay bond and furniture for any house he moves into.

I think the first time I sent Jamie off on his own to buy something was at McDonald's. He was about eight years old and I gave him a $10 note and asked him to buy chicken nuggets and chips. I waited outside, but I could tell, when his turn came, that something was going wrong. I went inside and the assistant was asking him what sauce he wanted with them. He didn't know what to reply. And then I realised that the purchase of goods in stores is so open-ended, the dialogue so loose that it was impossible to predict what the assistant would ask you. It would be many years before Jamie could go into a shop on his own and ask for goods, but that didn't stop us trying.

Now let's turn to the value of money. Here things are not so cut and dried. It's not a case of whether a 50 per cent discount is better than a 40 per cent discount or how much change you get from $10, but what our attitude is to money. And there it has to be an opinion, a value judgement. So what I have to say on the subject is my own personal view and may certainly differ from what anyone else believes.

First, I believe that money shouldn't be used as an inducement to do chores. I never paid Jamie or my other children to do work around the home. They got their pocket money – a modest amount every Saturday – and if they did something wrong, they could lose some of it, but they were never given more for good deeds. I reason that doing domestic chores is part of living in a family and working together – it's not a job that is negotiable. And the chores became more demanding as they got older.

As for pocket money, I never let the children buy sweets, chocolates, candy or lollies with it. I reasoned here that they weren't allowed to fritter it away or ruin their teeth. They'd have to save up for something decent (like a DVD or a book) so it helped with the saving mentality. As far as sweets were concerned, I would choose to buy them or not buy them when we were going shopping. I worked out a rather tricky modus operandi: if they asked for sweets, they definitely wouldn't get them. If they didn't say anything, they had a chance of my remembering to get them something.

Also from early on, I told Jamie about taxes. I wanted him to realise that taxation meant that we could all enjoy the benefits of a democratic government – so I'd say, 'Some of my pay goes to the government.' 'They give us the police, hospitals, schools, roads and laws.' 'So taxes are good.' Unfortunately, after a long time of these repetitions, he would say (to anyone who was talking about money), 'I want to pay taxes.' But when he left school and didn't have a job, I found him very upset one evening and he said, 'I don't have tax money!'

When Jamie did get a job at the age of 17, he was earning about $140 a week. He spent some of that money on sweets, but most of it he added to his savings and spent it on DVDs and computer games. Once he was earning, I made sure he chose and paid for any gifts for family members on their birthdays and at Christmas. He had to save up often to get what he wanted and never asked to borrow money from me or, worse, got involved in petty thieving. Overall, he understands the concepts of payment and earnings, has clear goals about saving and purchasing, and more than that, is honest, hardworking and generous.

Tips

Buy your child a coin box with an LED money counter in the lid.

Practise counting money at home and use cash as often as possible in shops.

Open a bank account with your child as soon as they are able to understand.

Reinforce mathematical concepts that they are being taught at school.

Be clear about what your values are about money, saving and finance and teach them actively.

CHAPTER 37

Noticing the Absence of Meltdowns and Encouraging Resilience

Yesterday was a milestone. Yesterday something happened that never happens – Caitlin got angry and Jamie didn't. It's was as unremarkable as that. Yet to me it was a triumph of the first order.

We headed into the city to get Caitlin to her semi-formal (an evening on board a paddle steamer) but we arrived five minutes late. Caitlin stormed out of the car, swearing that we had missed the boat and we might as well go home, and Jamie and I followed. I was dreading Jamie's reaction. He always became upset when Caitie was angry, caustic, grief-stricken or whatever. Whenever she lashes out – against her teachers, friends, enemies, the world or the TV – he can't follow what she's saying but he recognises the emotion and overheats himself.

So there I was in the middle of the city at night, parked on a double yellow line, with the very strong possibility that Jamie would run screaming and swearing off into the streetscape. As I did my best to calm Caitie and ask for directions from a passer-by, I kept an eye out for Jamie. He just followed and kept his peace. I was so grateful.

Of course, the boat hadn't left and we found the teachers waiting at the dock for late-comers and once Caitlin was heading down the gangplank, she was smiling as sweetly as an angel from Heaven, thanking me and giggling.

Phew!

I turned back to Jamie and immediately thanked him. We got in the car and I continued to praise him. I praised him for not saying anything, for not getting upset like his sister, for not presenting me with an extra difficulty, for refusing to get angry. I congratulated him from the bottom of my heart and awarded him five extra points, telling him it was due to his maturity.

A few weeks later we were off to Jamie's regular tennis lesson on a Friday afternoon. I had enrolled him in tennis lessons for special kids earlier in the year and he was progressing well. The lessons took place on courts belonging to a private school and were attended by about four or five other Special Needs kids ranging from 12 to 18 years of age. As we drove there, he asked, 'What will I get if I do well?' I had fallen into the habit of rewarding him after his game of tennis a few times and he was now in the habit of receiving something.

'I don't know,' I said. 'It depends how well you do.'

With that, he entered the court with determination.

Poor Jamie! Nothing went well for him that afternoon. The coach was sending him balls to practise his forehand and he kept running too far towards the ball, too close to take a good shot. Time and again it happened and I could see him becoming more and more disheartened. His shoulders drooped and he clenched his racquet, but the more he tried, the worse his returns got.

Finally, he came off the court and we walked back to the car.

'How do you feel?' I asked.

'Not good,' he replied through clenched teeth.

'No,' I said. 'I can see that. You're feeling very disappointed with yourself, aren't you?'

'Yes,' he admitted.

'That's because you didn't do well this week.'

'Yes, that's right. I couldn't get it. I just couldn't get it.'

'Well, do you know what I saw?' I asked.

'What?'

'I saw a boy who tried and tried and tried. I saw a boy who got annoyed but didn't take it out on anyone else. Do you know what "take it out" means?'

'No,' said Jamie unsure whether this was going to get him a treat or not.

'It's an idiom. It means you didn't get angry with anyone else but yourself. You didn't shout or throw your racquet down or walk off the court. You didn't take it out on anyone else. And do you know what that is?'

'What?'

'That's being mature. Just like you in the city when Caitie was shouting. You didn't do anything. You're being mature and more than that, you're becoming resilient. That's a new word. Do you know what it means?'

'Er... No.'

'It means you come back again and again to try when you're failing. Even though you're failing.'

Jamie was back to smiling again.

I continued: 'Resilience is a really important skill in life. You'll need it as you grow up when you're an adult. Being resilient means that you can put up with things that are difficult. You can try to make things better but, even if they don't improve or you don't get better, you can show resilience. And resilient people are the ones who are happiest in life. They understand that they may not succeed all the time, but they're going to do their best again and again. And that's what you did. You tried. You failed. You tried again and you failed again. But you showed that you were resilient. So today you showed that you were mature and resilient and I'm going to give you two points for that.'

On the way home, I explained to him in more detail how I had watched him as he listened to the coach's instructions and tried to do his best, getting more and more frustrated and angry with himself. But he kept his anger to himself and continued trying.

I don't think you can ask any more of anyone.

Tips

It's always difficult to put your child in for sports activities, whether it be in competition or not. There is a strong chance they'll fail. Even if they are not competing against another person, they can see how a ball should be hit or how a shot should be taken. And they know when they've not reached the standard. We usually say, 'Never mind. You did your best' or 'Good try'. Instead of that, think of ways of truly congratulating them on what they did achieve. Give them a clear explanation of exactly what they did and why it is worth rewarding. The life skill of resilience is more valuable than any number of aces on the court.

Praise the calm. Recognise the behaviour you want repeated.

And make sure, when you tell your friends or family about the good behaviour, whatever it is – that your child is around and can hear you.

CHAPTER 38

Preparing Your Child for Job Interviews

When Jamie was about 12, I started getting respite care for him. This was organised by a welfare group called Centacare. They would do 'babysitting' in your home while you went out for a break or they would do 'skilling' where you, your child and their representative worked out what skills would be useful for your child to have and they prepared a programme for him. Over the four-year relationship we had with Centacare, I used them for taking Jamie out on fun trips like ten-pin bowling and skating so that I could get on with work, and also 'skilling' sessions where he learned to travel on the buses on his own, for example (see p.107).

The first steps to getting on the list included an interview with the representative and then later an interview with the representative and the carer. Basically, it was to see if the child and the carer felt good about each other. Once I knew this was going to happen, I realised that I could take advantage of the situation to prepare Jamie for more important interviews later in his life.

As we came up to the interview date, I started prepping Jamie. I explained that he would be meeting a couple of strangers and refreshed his memory on how to meet and greet someone. But I also explained that this was an interview, and he had to behave particularly well. That included not fidgeting, not yawning, making eye contact, sitting and smiling, answering questions and trying to pay attention. He was awful in that first interview, looking away, trying to suppress yawns, laying his head on the table. But this was an ideal opportunity for me to give feedback.

I spoke to him afterwards and coached him on how to improve. As time went by, there were more opportunities for 'interviews' – student–teacher interviews, interviews with visiting teachers, interviews with employment consultants. I found these last ones the most useful because Jamie was asked direct questions about his activities, interests and hopes for the future. Also, they were interviews that I could sit in on and give Jamie feedback about. Each time he asked me afterwards how he had done, I always focused on his achievements.

Jamie's employment consultant came from an organisation that specialised in finding work for people with disabilities. They offered help in terms of job applications, but also attended job interviews with their clients and helped with on-the-job training and subsidies for employers for a set period of time. Once Jamie got on their books, he had to have fortnightly meetings and these again proved useful rehearsals for real job interviews.

One of his consultants was called Manny. He was a likeable, friendly chap who always engaged Jamie directly in conversation. He accompanied Jamie on two or three job interviews. At times Jamie would say something inappropriate and Manny would 'cover' for him, explaining that Jamie was just repeating something he had heard in a film. We both explained to Jamie that job interviews start with 'small talk' about the weather or the trip there. Then they lead to discussion on the hours and responsibilities, sometimes a tour of the premises. And at the end, there was the familiar shaking hands and thanks. This whole process helped Jamie construct a framework for the interview and helped him predict what was going to happen.

It was difficult but after several job interviews, Jamie landed a part-time job at a nursery. I was there for the interview and was so proud when Jamie rose to leave, shook hands with the boss and said, 'Thank you very much for seeing me. I hope I hear from you soon.'

Tips

Enrol your child with an agency which specialises in helping people with disabilities. They are experts in finding work for your child.

Take advantage of every opportunity to practise 'interviews'.

Explain the three stages of interviews: greeting and small talk, explanations and questions, farewell and thanks.

CHAPTER 39

Preparing Your Child for Driving

When I thought of Jamie's future, as he was growing up, I realised that his best options would be in unskilled work. Even so, I scoured the internet for typing training software, and got him started on a programme that taught him touch typing. I had no idea what Jamie would do in life, but I thought typing could always turn out to be a useful skill. Jamie resented the nightly practice but he did get up to 22 wpm and learnt all the finger placements.

At the same time, I encouraged him to take the online theoretical tests for driving. In Australia, you have to take a 30-question multiple choice test and there are hundreds of possible questions online that you can take in batches of 30. Each school night, in addition to homework, Jamie had to do his typing practice and complete one driving test. Pretty soon he became adept at the tests, and I considered taking him to the driving centre to take one.

Since it cost $90 a time to sit the Learner's Test, I waited until Jamie was regularly getting 30 out of 30 for his practise results, then booked his test and went along with him to the centre. There he was given a laminated sheet of questions and an answer sheet on which to mark his answers. He stood at the back of the room, seemingly getting more and more annoyed. I could see his frustration and considered moving towards him as there were queues of people milling around. Finally, I did go up to him and I saw immediately that he was circling his answers on the laminated sheet, which wouldn't take the biro marks. I quickly showed him the correct answer sheet and slid away.

He failed.

A month later we went back again. He failed again. A month later we went back again. He failed again. Each time I stood by him as he got his results and a patient clerk explained to him how he had failed and which questions he'd got wrong. After the fourth time of failing, Jamie said to me, 'Why do I have to do this test?' And I answered, 'Because it's worth it.'

To me, it was. Jamie had become quite intrigued by the Learner's tests online and regularly set himself the tests for truck drivers as well as car drivers. He learnt the difference between medium rigid and heavy rigid trucks and showed such an interest, I could see he was envisaging a future of truck driving for himself. I didn't want to push it on him, but it seemed a natural progression.

The Learner's Test questions were divided into two parts – ten questions on Give Way situations and 20 questions on general knowledge of road rules and signs. Jamie always got 10/10 for the Give Way questions as they involved graphics and maps, but the general knowledge was always difficult for him. I remember one surprise question on the test was: 'How far apart may cyclists ride on a standard two-way road?' I doubt Jamie understood the question let alone knew the answer. So it was his comprehension that always let him down.

At the fifth test, when he failed again, the clerk suggested that he help Jamie next time to clarify what the questions mean and see if he could make the English understandable. I was very grateful, but at Jamie's sixth go, he waved away help from the attendants and boldly placed his answer sheet down for correction.

He passed!

At the sixth go he had passed the theory test for driving. We were thrilled. I took him out to his favourite restaurant to celebrate and he casually waved his Learner's driving licence in front of the waiter's nose as we ordered. I explained to the surprised waiter that this was a celebratory dinner as Jamie had passed his theory driving test.

Then, of course, followed the practical driving lessons that sparked in me such anxiety. First, I enrolled Jamie with a driving school, explaining to the receptionist that Jamie had particular problems and asking her to suggest the best, most patient instructor for him. She recommended Dennis and Jamie warmed to him immediately, basically because he was quiet and firm.

I went with Jamie on his first lesson to help Dennis learn how to communicate with Jamie (simple instructions, basic words, showing not telling, etc.). I was terrified! Even though the car was dual operation and Jamie was only driving up and down a culvert, I was absolutely petrified. I fled from the car at the end of the lesson, hardly able to thank Dennis and arrange the next lesson.

So Jamie continued his lessons for a while but then wanted to have practice sessions in my car. I said he could do so once he'd worked up 20 hours in Dennis's car. It was just an excuse to defer the date. Eventually, I had to give in and buy the 'L' plates and accompany Jamie on his driving. I deliberately took him to the flattest, least populated area I could think of and we simply practised moving off after checking the blind spot and then parking.

Every trip I made with Jamie, I was frightened. I simply held my fear inside me and shut my mouth, thinking to myself, 'I want Jamie to learn to drive. This is the only way to do it.'

Exactly one year to the day after he got his Learner's licence, Jamie passed his practical test. It was his first attempt.

Tips

Sound out your youngster on their attitude to cars and driving.

Encourage then if they want to take the tests and put your fear in your pocket.

Help them get used to the tests by doing examples online.

Spend time choosing a suitable instructor.

CHAPTER 40

Preparing for the First Day at Work

Jamie was very lucky in his later school years: he had a dedicated teacher who was determined to get him work experience positions that were as varied as possible. These jobs were unskilled part-time positions for periods of about four to six weeks. They included: storeman unpacking books in a book store, video checkout assistant, library assistant and retail stockist at The Endeavour Foundation charity.

Jamie was well suited to the work – a lot of it was unpacking or restocking the shelves. He has always enjoyed putting things in order. In several cases, he wanted to continue the work but the employers maintained that they wanted to offer the same opportunities to other young people with similar disabilities.

In two cases, I was instrumental in getting Jamie the job – at the charity and the book store. I approached the charity directly and asked them if they could use some help in their retail store, then, when they accepted, I put them in touch with the school to arrange it. With the book store, I heard from a mother of a school friend of Jamie's that this book store offered work placements to teenagers with disabilities and I simply passed the information on to Jamie's teacher. The point is that it's a good idea to keep your mind open to possible work openings – talk to friends, parents, teachers and even approach organisations or small businesses on your own.

The other point to remember is to choose something that your child is likely to succeed at. There is nothing more demoralising to your child than placing them in a workplace doing a job they fail at. Shayne, Jamie's teacher, was well aware of this and made sure that Jamie's positions were well within his capabilities, like matching the books to the Hold Requests and placing them in alphabetical order or reshelving videos in the video shop.

Charity work is also a good option – Jamie worked for The Endeavour Foundation for three years for three hours a week. He had to tidy up the toys, sort out the books and unpack the new stock. Later I rang a few charity depots where they collected and delivered furniture to disadvantaged families. Because of Jamie's love of driving, he was delighted to be accompanying the driver of the truck on his rounds.

Before each work placement, I drove Jamie to the place in our free time. If he was going to get there by bus, we did the trip that way. I talked about how long the trip would take, what the landmarks were, how he could tell when to get off or where to park. I also checked up on what he should wear – sometimes black shirt and trousers were required so I had Jamie lay out the right uniform the night before so he wouldn't get confused.

Before his first day, I made sure I knew the name of the contact person at the job and I got him to practise saying it, as in: 'Good morning, Steve. Where do I put my jacket?' 'Hello, Gayle. It's a nice day, isn't it?' I'm not sure that Jamie ever followed my advice – he's always had difficulty saying people's names to their faces – but the feedback from each job was positive, with the employers saying that Jamie was friendly and hardworking, if slow.

Try to think of as many things as you can that will affect your child's working day and what they need to know beforehand: when will they have lunch, do they have to bring it themselves, where will they eat, how many breaks will they have and when, do they have to fit in with other employees? But, as much as you can try to manage their job beforehand, your child is the one who will have to respond spontaneously to situations that are beyond your control. All you can do is try to get feedback from the employer and the teacher/employment consultant.

For now is the time to let go...

Tips

Choose jobs that are suited to your child's capabilities.

Keep your ear out for jobs that other children have got.

Prepare your child by following the route to the job on public transport if necessary.

Get your child to practise the names of the employers beforehand.

Be positive about your child's successes and go through their day with them afterwards.

Believe in them.

Afterword

Where Are We Now?

So how is Jamie doing now? Well, he's 18 years old and has a part-time job at a wholesale plant nursery. He got the job through a friend of his at school and now works there two days a week. He is so proud of the money he gets through his work and enjoys preparing his lunch for the following day. When he comes back each night, he complains about how dirty he is and rushes to the shower, but it's clear he loves the messy sweat of hard toil and feels 'like a man'.

He has been working there for a year now and they have accepted him as a hardworking, happy co-worker. The nursery tends plants on factory production lines and Jamie takes part in the end process of loading the plants for transport to retail outlets. He uses an industrial stapler to staple cardboard boxes together or tags each pot with a bar code or sticks the care instructions in the soil, so it's not a horticultural job as much as packaging the finished product.

His other major achievement, which has eased our lives incredibly, is his driving. After failing so many times at the theory test, he was delighted to pass his practical at the first go. Then a few months later, he got himself a car. This was done with the money I'd been saving for him since he was born. He had more than enough to buy a modest second-hand manual car (I wanted him to consolidate his experience with manuals – mine is an automatic), pay for the insurance, registration, car breakdown service and regular servicing.

Now he can go shopping for himself to buy clothes, shoes and so on, without having to go with me. He purchases the goods and I pay him back. He can also get himself to the nursery, which lies almost an hour's drive away from our house. Having a car also prompted him to think about night-time entertainment and pretty soon he was asking me if he could go to a pub.

This was a whole new ball game. I didn't know how to respond. At first he said he wanted to go to the pub every night. I quickly dispelled that idea, saying that he couldn't go out every night but perhaps once or twice a week. Then there was the question of which pub. He insisted on a sordid area in the inner city which was notorious for its police raids, drug busts and binge-drinking sessions. I managed to persuade him that a pub nearer to us and beside the local university would be more appropriate.

So now Jamie goes to the Royal Exchange every Wednesday night, where he dances and dances. They've even put pictures of him up on their Facebook page. He doesn't even drink, having decided that alcohol is dangerous. This suits me fine. He always tells me when he'll be home and keeps to that schedule.

On the days that he doesn't work, he either 'has a break', which means he plays computer or Xbox games, or he goes to the gym in the city. He joined up and goes there twice a week, feeling very healthy.

Jamie also does charity work. I think it's a great idea if you can find work that suits your child. Jamie is very interested in trucks so I arranged for Jamie to work at the St Vincent de Paul's depot, collecting and delivering furniture, giving the guys in the big trucks a hand. He loves travelling around the city in the van and giving people their 'new' furniture.

Is there anything I would change in Jamie's life? Well, certainly, I wish he had closer ties to his friends. He won't take the first step and invite someone out to the cinema or into town. Neither will he put himself forward to any of the girls he meets at the Royal Exchange. But whenever I try to suggest some course of action related to socialising, he just says, 'Mum, that's for me to think about. I'll decide.'

And now that he's doing so well, I think that it's time for me to step back and accept that the next step's for him to take.

A Conversation with Jamie

I had the following conversation with Jamie in July 2013 when he was 18 years old and had been working at the nursery for over a year.

'Do you remember me beginning to talk to you about conversation?'
'Yes, I was a little rascal. You remember telling me what's important – it's having a conversation. We've got to listen, talk and think before we take part in a conversation.'

'Do you think conversation is important? Why?'
'Yes, conversation is important because it's better to explain than resorting to anything horrible and bad.'

'How has conversation training helped you?'
'I felt like I wanted to talk to friends that didn't have any disabilities so I decided to meet people who were very good at talking and who could help me make conversations.'

'Do you remember getting angry with the teachers at school?'
'Yes, at my old school they weren't explaining the right way, which made me realise that I had to do better than being an Aspie.'

'Does it upset you being an Aspie?'
'Not really upset, just a bit disappointed. Yes, it makes me different sometimes.'

'Do you remember getting angry with Caitie?'
'Yep. Lots of times. Having words made it easier for me – not getting so angry.'

'What got you most angry when you were younger?'
'If I had a guess. I'd say listening to you and Caitie fight again and again.'

'What do you think of your life now?'
'It's getting better and I'm doing the best I can and I'm getting very good at communicating with other people, but I get disappointed when the interview people don't ring back.'

Appendix

Measuring Your Child's Progress

In a recent book I read on marketing (Seth Godwin's *The Purple Cow*), the author stated that we can't know where we've got to if we can't measure the change. This table measures your child's growth and development in the areas of conversation, behaviour, socialisation and life skills.

Complete the upper part of the chart with your child's name, age (in years and months), date, hearing ability and their active vocabulary. To find their active vocabulary, you will have to note down the number of different words they can generate. For example, 'ice-cream', 'go', 'never', 'won't', and 'yes' are five separate words on the vocabulary list.

Read the abilities on the left and put a tick or cross next to each one as you decide whether your child has achieved that milestone or not. Then for every cross on the chart, work consistently on that ability with your child one-to-one (in the car while travelling is the best place for this). Finally, when your child achieves that milestone, proudly write the date in the column on the right.

Name: _____

Age: _____

Date: _____

Can hear properly? Has had a hearing test? _____

Has an active vocabulary of how many words? (Make a list on a seperate piece of paper)

Achievement	Tick or cross for ability to perform this action and date	Date achieved
Responds to own name		
Can ask a simple Yes/ No question to find out information		
Can ask a simple 'Wh-' question as part of active listening to your statements		
Can ask a simple Yes/No question as part of active listening to your statements		
Will make empathetic sentences (e.g. 'Oh, no, that's sad.')		
Can put simple sentences together (e.g. 'I like this.')		

Achievement	Tick or cross for ability to perform this action and date	Date achieved
Stops babbling nonsense when requested		
Asks permission to interrupt		
Knows when it's their turn to speak		
Knows when it's their turn to listen		
Complies 80% of the time when you ask for eye contact		
Understands the reward system you have chosen		
Demands use of the reward system to reward their behaviour		
Can take part in simple exchanges of phatic communication		
Can use and remember people's names		
Introduces people's names in conversation		
Can understand your use of body language terminology		
Can identify the main character(s) in a film and name them		

Can retell a simple storyline from a book or a film		
Can repeat small extracts of text from a poem or song		
Can understand/use the word 'idiom'		
Can identify common idioms in other people's speech		
Can use common idioms in own speech		
Responds positively to praise		
Can make own breakfast with supervision		
Can prepare own school lunch with supervision		
Can make own bed with supervision		
Can estimate own temper level on a visual thermometer		
Can make own breakfast		
Can prepare own school lunch		
Can make own bed		
Can take part in role-plays		
Can go through a debrief of a crisis and learn key concepts from it		
Can understand and accept the rules of simple games		
Can play card or board games and be a gracious loser		

Achievement	Tick or cross for ability to perform this action and date	Date achieved
Can accept disappointment in changed arrangements		
Can interpret non-interest in listener		
Can accept non-interest in listener and change topic		
Can follow a regular routine		
Can accept changes from a regular routine		
Can perform simple chores around the house		
Can help you compile a shopping list		
Can help you locate groceries when shopping		
Can prepare or combine ingredients for cooking		
Can prepare simple dishes with supervision		
Can prepare simple dishes without supervision		
Can understand the concept of 'maturity'		

Has developed the attitude of maturity in most of their relationships		
Can understand the concept of 'resilience'		
Has developed the skills of resilience		
Can understand the concept of 'independence'		
Has developed the skills of independence		

Recommended Resources

Books

Gardner, N. (2007) *A Friend Like Henry*. Hodder and Stoughton: London.
Jackson, L. (2002) *Freaks, Geeks and Asperger Syndrome: A User Guide to Adolescence*. London: Jessica Kingsley Publishers.
Robinson, J. E. (2011) *Be Different: Adventures of a Free-Range Aspergian with Practical Advice for Aspergians, Misfits, Families and Teachers*. Ontario: Doubleday.

Films

Quantum of Solace (2008) Directed by Marc Forster. Eon Productions.
Rain Man (1988) Directed by Barry Levinson. United Artists.
Seven Up! (1964) Directed by Paul Almond. ITV.
Terminator (1984) Directed by James Cameron.

Index

Page numbers in *italics* refer to figures.